Pluto 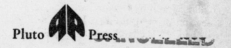 Press

The Politics of Health

Editor: Lesley Doyal

Pluto's new series on the politics of health will be concerned with social and environmental causes of ill-health both here and in the third world. It will look at the growing critique of contemporary medical practice as well as the possibility of socialist and feminist alternatives for the creation of a healthy society.

First published 1981 by Pluto Press Limited,
Unit 10 Spencer Court, 7 Chalcot Road, London NW1 8LH

ISBN 0 86104 341 3

Cover designed by Clive Challis
Cover photograph by Trefor Ball
Photoset and printed in Great Britain by Photobooks
(Bristol) Ltd, 28 Midland Road, St Philips, Bristol.

Contents

To all the women who have nearly stopped smoking

Acknowledgements

There are so many people I want to thank I hardly know where to start. I am enormously indebted to ASH for opening its offices to me, and to Patti White in particular for answering my unending series of questions with both patience and accuracy. Mike Daube has been an invaluable source of ideas and support. His comments and meticulous eye for detail helped the book to evolve at every stage. I benefited greatly from Susan Berlin's sharp and perceptive ideas, and Ann Oakley's careful comments helped to give me a broader perspective. Despite substantial differences of opinion, I want to thank Beulah Bewley for her helpful criticism at various stages of writing. I especially want to thank Lesley Doyal and Eva Kaluzynska, my editors, whose extraordinary whittling powers, combined with enthusiastic support, helped to improve the book so much. Thanks, too, to Freddi Cooke, Beryl Frost, Wendy Willmott, Suzanne Dolly and Avis Levene for typing a virtually illegible manuscript.

There are many people in the USA, Canada and elsewhere who have invested much time and effort into providing me with large amounts of valuable information—especially Kurt Baumgartner of the Canadian Council on Smoking and Health, William Forbes of the University of Waterloo, Jerry Schwarz of the University of California at Davis, and the American Cancer Society. My friends have been a constant source of support. Jonathan Evans' friendship and love helped to give me the confidence to stop smoking in 1973. Judy Breuer patiently tolerated my nocturnal writing habits for too long. Milena Boyle's energy propelled me through my moments of lowest ebb, and Mike Durham's ability to prise me away from my typewriter helped to preserve my sanity.

I could not have written this book were it not for all the women—smokers and ex-smokers alike—who gave me the opportunity to learn so much about what smoking means to women. I am grateful to Martin Raw and Howard Williams who put me in touch with women smokers through their clinics. Above all, I owe a great deal to Jane, Valerie and Aileen who—despite suffering life-threatening and disabling illnesses—were prepared to give me so much of their precious time.

Bobbie Jacobson

Introduction

Why a book on women and smoking? Surely smoking affects both men and women. Cigarette smoking does indeed kill about four times as many men as women each year. But women are rapidly gaining ground, each year coming closer to an equality in death that most never achieve in life. Men are giving up, yet women are smoking more heavily than ever before. If current trends continue, women could take over from men next century as the main victims of the cigarette.

I became interested in the problem of women smokers while working for ASH (Action on Smoking and Health) in London. I noticed that about three-quarters of the requests we received each week from smokers who desperately wanted to stop were from women. At the same time I was surprised at how little any of the 'experts' seemed to know about Britain's nine million women smokers. At the launch of the third Royal College of Physicians' Report, *Smoking* or *Health* in 1977, a woman journalist asked the male medical panel why it was that smoking was rising among women. Only one member responded, to admit he had no idea.

When I started to write this book, I did not see the problem in a feminist light at all, but my work on it convinced me that smoking was very much a feminist issue. As a problem, it has been ignored not only by a predominantly male medical profession, but by women's organisations too. Many 'experts' on smoking and health met my questions about women smokers with sheer evasion or even defensiveness bordering on acrimony. Health educators and researchers do not normally study sex differences in smoking patterns, nor do they consult women when planning campaigns directed at women smokers, having assumed that what works for men will work for women. It is an indictment of both men and women involved in the preventive health field that we had to wait until 1980 to see the publication of the US Surgeon-General's findings on women and smoking, the first major report that treats the problem with the seriousness it deserves.

I was even more disturbed by the lack of priority that women's organisations—feminist or otherwise—give to the problem. A few expressed a mild interest, but most considered it to be strictly a non-issue. Meanwhile the tobacco industry continues to exploit women and to make every effort to expand the already massive female market.

The purpose of this book is to examine the smoking problem as it relates to women and to describe the dilemma that now faces so many women smokers. I have divided the book into two parts. In the first I try to build up a picture of why women smoke. The second part deals with the business of stopping. For those who want to read further, I have included a list of references at the end of the book.

I have deliberately concentrated on the differences between male and female smoking habits, for they provide the key to understanding why more women are smoking than ever before. Of course, not all women (or all smokers) behave in the same way, which is why I let individual women I spoke to describe the particular problems they encountered. I hope women readers will find something of themselves in the book. Any discussion of differences in the way men and women behave inevitably raises the thorny issue of whether there are innate psychological differences between the sexes. In the absence of any good evidence of such differences, I have concentrated on the social and economic factors that so obviously make the lives of most women different from those of most men. Before going on, it seems important to make my own experience and interests clear. I am a woman, and my perspective is, therefore, different from that of most people (men) running the smoking and health campaign. For me the justification for this book lies in the incontrovertible evidence that cigarettes kill more relatively young people from heart attacks, lung cancer and chronic chest illnesses than any other single cause. I am not an evangelist. Cigarette smoking to me is not a sin—it is a health hazard. I am an ex-smoker of long enough standing to have grown out of the self-righteousness which plagues many of us for a short while. While I have myself campaigned for the rights of the non-smoker, I have little sympathy with the crusaders who feel the urge to purge society of smokers. This does little more than increase feelings of guilt among smokers—most of whom want to stop anyway.

All the women's accounts, which follow, are true; I have

changed their names to protect their privacy. I make no apology for focusing on the ill health cigarettes cause in women, and hope to help destroy the myth that lung cancer and heart disease are a male preserve.

My education in biochemistry and my current medical training have taught me to draw as much as I can from the scientific literature on smoking. But my observations also come from impressions I have acquired from women who had the patience to discuss their smoking problems with me.

I. The Sexual Politics of Smoking: Why Women Smoke

1. A Tale of Four Women

Jill is almost there

Jill is *almost* a model ex-smoker. There are no ashtrays or cigarettes in her flat. Her office is filled with anti-smoking posters, and she would not dream of travelling in a smoking compartment on the underground. She has even persuaded several friends to stop smoking. Yet the notice that greets you on her front door betrays a trace of the lingering doubt in her mind: 'THIS IS *SUPPOSED* TO BE A NO SMOKING ZONE. WE ARE TRYING TO GIVE UP SMOKING. YOUR HELP WOULD BE APPRECIATED.' Although Jill effectively stopped smoking six months ago, she still sees herself as a part-time ex-smoker waiting patiently to experience 'that lovely confident feeling you have when you *know* the craving is completely gone.'

Jill has never had any doubts about the dangers of cigarettes. She even remembers trying to persuade her parents to stop smoking when she was ten. 'I was so frightened about their smoking. I used to hear them both cough every morning until they retched. In those days they called it "Smoker's Cough", but I knew that I didn't *ever* want to cough like that.' Yet Jill learned to smoke like other children of her age.

'Smoking was very much the grown up thing to do. I felt very isolated unless I did likewise.' Smoking was a game to Jill and her friends who lived on a farm. 'We used to collect the farm labourer's fag ends, dry out the tobacco, and roll our own cigarettes with Bronco toilet paper.'

When Jill was 18 she met a New Zealander, Mark, who was to become her husband. Life went well for them until she became pregnant, married him, and went out to New Zealand to live with him. At that stage she was still only smoking occasionally. Things went rapidly downhill from her arrival in New Zealand. 'Mark became bored with me very quickly, because I was pregnant and no longer able to have sex—the last thing I wanted when I was being sick every morning. And the one thing that had really held us together was the sex.'

After her twins were born, Jill's despair grew: 'I was deeply unhappy. I was 4,000 miles away from home and there was no-one to talk to. My husband was never there. He was either out with another woman, or drinking with friends. The only way I could cope was to become a mechanical mother—technically perfect, but anaesthetised. My own feelings were so painful I couldn't afford to feel them.'

Stuck at home with the babies, Jill found herself rapidly transforming from an occasional to a heavy smoker. 'Smoking helped to dampen things down. When it got to the stage when I couldn't bear it any longer, I found if I lit up a cigarette it helped to get me over the next five minutes. It gave me enough breathing space to stop the endless crying, and carry on with whatever had to be done. There was no way, at that time, that I could have coped without cigarettes: it was that or alcohol.'

After two years Jill left Mark and returned to England with her twins. She was, by then, smoking more than 30 cigarettes a day. Mark followed her and they spent a further stormy year together, during which time she became pregnant again. 'The whole thing was a nightmare. He was always screwing other women and bringing them back here. He would humiliate me in a thousand ways. One minute he'd tell me about the prostitutes and men he was sleeping with, and then he'd say: Now I want my conjugal rights.' He was spiteful, so I was spiteful back. The only way I could get at him was to verbally emasculate him. I used to go on and on until he hit me. Once he actually kicked me when I was three or four months pregnant. I started to bleed, and it was touch and go as to whether I'd miscarry. Eventually Susan was born two months premature.'

Jill continued to rely heavily on cigarettes throughout this period. It was not until several years later—after she and Mark were divorced—that she began to think seriously about giving up smoking. Life had changed radically. She was coping well with three young children. She had a new job as a secretary/administrator at a polytechnic, and was happily living with a man. But she began to worry about her health and the niggling cough she'd developed. 'Living with Tim—who was a lot younger than me – made me aware of myself through my sexuality. Seeing myself as a desirable woman made me realise that I needed to invest a little

4

more care and concern in my body. Tim and I used to do a lot of sport together and I'd always considered myself pretty fit and healthy. That's why it was such a shock to me when I couldn't make it up the stairs, when I saw him pounding away ahead of me . . . I began to notice that if the lift was broken I couldn't get up to the flat without stopping at every landing for breath. It really appalled me that at my age, 32, it took a few stairs to suffocate me. If I went to visit friends who didn't have a lift, I'd have to walk very slowly up the stairs, and it would take me about twenty minutes to recover. I became terribly conscious of the permanent fur rug on my tongue. Real Wilton. And the dirt. I began to notice that too. Every morning when I got up the flat stank. Ashtrays were filled with fags and the wallpaper and paintwork was coated with this horrible yellow gunge.'

One night, after relentlessly smoking her way through 25 cigarettes, she made up her mind to give up. She left the smouldering pyramid of cigarette ends in the ashtray for three weeks to remind her of her decision. Despite finding it a real effort, Jill was thrilled with her success: 'I began to feel very good about myself. I found I could run all the way up the stairs without getting puffed, and I could play a decent game of squash again. And one of the most extraordinary things was the rediscovery of my sense of taste – the fur completely disappeared from my tongue!' Things were looking up at work as well: Jill became involved in the research work in her department. 'I felt as though I was really developing as a person. I think I felt more confident then than at any time in my life.'

But her confidence was eroded as her relationship with Tim ended and she began to feel dissatisfied at work. She applied for upgrading and felt disillusioned and betrayed when her colleagues did not back her up. 'I felt bitter and exploited. They were getting more and more promotion, but I was still the "typist". I think this reverberation in both my emotional and working life pushed me gradually back to depending on cigarettes.' At first Jill 'borrowed' cigarettes from other people. She felt she could continue to regard herself as a non-smoker as long as she didn't buy cigarettes herself. But her borrowing rate grew embarrassingly and she finally had to admit that, after three years off cigarettes, she had become a smoker again.

After several further unsuccessful attempts to stop, things began to look hopeful again for Jill. 'I had readjusted myself to survival at work and no longer expected support from my colleagues. I began to look into other facilities at work that could make my life more palatable.' Jill gradually became more active within her local trade union, and signed on for a Diploma in Women's Studies. As new opportunities—including the possibility of doing full-time research—presented themselves, she slowly regained some of her lost confidence. Six months ago Jill felt ready to face life without cigarettes. She put out her last cigarette on her 42nd birthday. Or so she thought. The trouble is she still feels a niggling, occasionally overwhelming need to have the odd cigarette. Jill recognises from experience that she could easily slip back into heavy smoking. Yet at the same time she feels hopeful about becoming a *full-time* ex-smoker at last.

Aileen has had a heart attack

A massive heart attack at 47 followed by open heart surgery ten years later was not enough to keep Aileen off cigarettes. 'I used to believe you could stop at any time, but I now know that the best solution is never to buy any cigarettes at all. I did manage to stop for ten whole days after the operation, but that was only because the first thing the doctor said when I came round from the anaesthetic was: "If you carry on smoking you will die." But when I was back at home with nothing to do but lie in bed all day, I eventually said to myself: you might as well have a cigarette.' And so Aileen slowly crept back to 20 cigarettes a day.

It never crossed Aileen's mind that cigarettes might make her ill. 'I'd never had any chest trouble so I thought I'd got away with it.' Like many of her contemporaries, Aileen was raised on 40 untipped cigarettes—the most dangerous kind—a day, which she had smoked for more than 30 years. 'In those days,' says Aileen, 'nobody knew that smoking was bad for you.'

Aileen's heart trouble caught her unawares in the middle of the night while her husband was away at sea: 'I didn't know what had hit me: it felt as if somebody had shoved a brick down my throat. I managed to crawl out of bed, but fell on the landing before I could get to the phone. I was really frightened: my whole chest felt as if it were bursting out. I was gasping and everything was swimming. And the pain: it was the worst pain I'd ever had. The pain of having my children was nothing by comparison. I still remember the whole ordeal as if it were yesterday. I must have blacked out because I remember coming to, and asking the ambulance man for a cigarette. He said: you're too ill to smoke. I was pretty disgusted with myself. I thought: God I'm dying and all I can think of is a cigarette.'

After six weeks' recuperation, Aileen went back to her job as a school cook, still smoking 40 cigarettes a day. Her troubles soon returned. She began to experience increasingly frequent episodes of angina, a crushing pain in the chest brought on by exertion. Her doctor put her on a special low cholesterol diet, and was very direct in his advice to her about smoking: 'Why should the health service spend money on you when you can't even help yourself to stop smoking?' The tablets he prescribed helped the pain at first, but the angina steadily worsened and became unbearable over the next two years. 'At first I used to get it walking up hills, but it eventually got so bad that I couldn't even walk 50 yards to the bus stop to catch the bus to work—they had to send a taxi to come and collect me. Everything gave me a pain: I couldn't lift any-thing. I couldn't even bend down to make the beds. I was totally useless . . .

'Sometimes you would wake up in the middle of the night feeling all queer and breathless. Other times you couldn't lie down flat at all. I became frightened of going to bed. I used to think I might slip away in the night. Each time I woke up the next morning, I'd say thank God I'm still alive.'

Eventually the doctors decided that the only way of relieving Aileen's disabling and life-threatening pain was to perform major open heart surgery in which they replaced the blocked arteries in her heart with a vein from her leg. Aileen now has a seven inch tramline scar down her chest and left leg to remind her of what she has been through. Although her chest pain has gone, Aileen's past has taken its inevitable toll. She has been off work for more than a year, and the £26 a week she receives in sickness benefit is hardly enough to make ends meet after paying £16 a week in rent. 'I don't think I could face going back to work now,' she says. 'Although I badly miss the company, I just haven't got the stamina to do the work I used to do. I shall have to face the prospect of staying at home permanently now.'

Jane had Lung Cancer

At 47, Jane was very young and unlucky to have developed an inoperable lung cancer. Jane had never been in hospital before the tumour was diagnosed. She had always been very fit. Despite smoking up to 50 cigarettes a day, she didn't even have the familiar smoker's cough. Jane thought she was invulnerable to ill health. 'When I first saw the anti-smoking commercials of the early seventies, I remember being vaguely aware of the hazards, but not enough to do anything about it. Besides, I didn't think that what they said was necessarily true because I know loads of people who had smoked all their lives and lived to 80, and those who'd never smoked a cigarette in their lives and died of lung cancer. I took a fatalistic attitude, but I didn't seriously think it would happen to me.'

Following the diagnosis, Jane's attitude to her health changed abruptly: 'I'm now acutely aware of how precious good health is. You take it for granted until something like this happens. If I can get my health back with the treatment, I will give up cigarettes.'

Jane became ill quite suddenly about a year ago with what seemed like a mild stomach upset: 'I just didn't seem to get well again. I thought perhaps I needed a holiday. I lost a stone-and-a-half in weight and couldn't seem to regain it. I then noticed I was becoming utterly breathless. Simply going to the shops was enough to knock me out. On one or two occasions my colleagues at work simply had to grab my bags from me and sit me down because I was literally gasping. I wasn't unduly worried then because the doctor thought it was bronchitis with a touch of asthma. What really frightened me was when I coughed up blood. I realised it had to be something more serious than just asthma. That was when I went for a chest X-ray, and they found out what was really the trouble . . .'

'I wasn't as distressed as I thought I would be, although I was a bit shattered at the thought that suddenly I might not have a future. I'm not a very emotional person: I've never shed a tear since I've known about the tumour. My feelings come out in funny ways. Normally I can never resist buying a pair of shoes when I walk past a shoe shop, yet after the diagnosis I found I could resist easily as I no longer knew whether I'd be around for another six months to wear those shoes.' Since then, Jane had three courses of chemotherapy (injection of drugs to kill the tumour) and one course of radiotherapy over the last six months which meant regular hospital admissions.

Yet, the most difficult thing to cope with was not so much the illness itself, but her loss of independence: 'I've always been a very energetic and active person. I would dearly love to be back at work with my colleagues. I'm still keeping my fingers crossed that I will be able to go back. I used to do a lot of ballroom dancing. I can't dance at all now. When I see healthy people of my age dancing and running on TV, I feel very envious. I've had to stop doing all the other things I enjoy most. Ten minutes gardening makes me breathless enough to have to rest. But most of all I regret not being able to take the dog for a walk any more.' Jane is not at all bitter about the prospect of dying young: 'I simply try to accept the situation. I feel I'm lucky in a way to have had 45 good years. Some children die before they've even had a chance in life. I've had such a happy life. I have no unfulfilled ambitions—except perhaps hope.' Jane's condition deteriorated rapidly over the next few months. The tumour had spread to her liver. She died less than nine months after the diagnosis was made.

Valerie had Chronic Bronchitis

Smoking 20 cigarettes a day seemed perfectly normal to Valerie. Everyone smoked during the war. It never occurred to her that she might spend the following 30 years crippled by chronic bronchitis. By the time Valerie was 42 she was so disabled that she had to retire from her job as a waitress. Valerie's doctor says: 'There can be no doubt that her severe, chronic chest disease was a consequence of her heavy cigarette smoking.' Several doctors advised Valerie to stop smoking, but she says she didn't really take their warnings seriously. 'When I was younger I was too busy bringing up five children to worry about my health. I thought bronchitis was just a bit of a cough and irritation in your throat. I never imagined it could go down to your lungs and cause so much suffering. If I'd known then what I know now, I would have stopped smoking before it was too late.' (Valerie has been trying to stop smoking for years, but has resigned herself to six a day). 'I now know that I'm so bad that a few cigarettes a day can't possibly make me any worse.'

When Valerie and I met she had not been out for six months—except to the hospital. At 55 she could no longer climb the stairs in her house and was confined to the settee in the living room. A large oxygen cylinder and a selection of tablets were her constant companions. The outer limits of Valerie's world stretched to the living room door—a mere five yards, beyond which she became too breathless to continue walking.

'I began to get very short of breath in my mid-thirties. I couldn't stop coughing. No medicines seemed to help. I just got worse and worse. I knew I was becoming really ill, yet I still carried on smoking. From the moment I wake up in the morning I can't breathe. I can't explain the horrible, frightening feeling you get when you are gasping for breath, and coughing and bringing up phlegm at the same time. I'm in and out of hospital all the time. I have to stay in hospital each time I get the slightest chill. My doctor has told me that there is nothing he can do to help. Sometimes, when I need the oxygen badly, I get so tight that no air will go into my lungs at all. I don't really mind the pain you get with chronic bronchitis, it's the panic of not being able to breathe—especially when I'm on my own—that is the worst. Sometimes I get so scared I can't even put the oxygen mask on.'

Valerie had an emergency operation for peritonitis after an infected part of the bowel burst into her abdomen which left her with a temporary colostomy, a section of bowel diverted and emptying into a bag attached to the outside of the abdomen. But Valerie's bronchitis was so severe that her lungs collapsed after the operation and she had to be put on a machine that breathed for her. Valerie's husband didn't think she would pull through. 'Even the doctors were surprised to see that I'd made it,' said Valerie. The surgeons couldn't close up and repair Valerie's colostomy because a further operation would almost certainly have killed her. So she was left to cope with a permanent colostomy: 'My husband and daughter have to fix it for me because I get too breathless bending down to empty it.' Like Jane, it was not so much the illness itself that depressed Valerie, but the enormous restrictions it imposed on her: 'My life has completely changed since I became ill. It literally broke my heart when I had to stop work. I now do nothing. I can't work. I can't cook. I can't go across to the shops or go for a walk in the park. I can't even sleep properly: I have to sleep sitting up with five pillows or I can't breathe at all. Being sentenced to sitting here all day makes me feel a burden to my family. I'm used to doing a lot of things for myself. Now I'm helpless. It takes a lot of getting used to. All I have left is to sit here on my own wondering what will happen to me, wondering if it will get worse.' A few months later it did. Valerie died of pneumonia.

2. Today's Epidemic

The proportion of men who smoke is going down in many industrialised countries, yet it is not easy to find a country where the same is true of women. In Britain, men seem to have responded to the anti-smoking campaigns of the last 15 years, so that the proportion of male smokers has decreased from nearly 60 per cent in 1961 to 47 per cent in 1975. Over the same period, the proportion of women smokers has remained unchanged at about 40 per cent.[1] Why? The reason for this discrepancy between men and women is twofold. First, men have stopped smoking in larger numbers than women and, second, fewer boys are now starting while the proportion of girls who start is increasing. So the *total* proportion of women smokers has hardly changed, because the women who have stopped have been cancelled out by the increasing numbers of young women recruited. Government surveys between 1978 and 1980 show that the smoking trend among women is, if anything, upward, while for men it continues to go down slowly.[2]

Not only is the *proportion* of women smokers increasing in many countries, but so also is the *amount* they smoke. Until the second world war, excessive 'indulgence' in cigarettes was considered unladylike and those who did smoke were expected not to inhale too deeply or to leave too short a stub. Indeed, keeping to feminine etiquette was probably partly responsible for holding down female lung-cancer rates until recently. In 1950 the average British woman got through half as many cigarettes as her male contemporary. Now, she has almost caught him up and smokes more than 15 cigarettes a day.[3] The story is similar elsewhere. In the USA, men are smoking only marginally more heavily than 25 years ago, but women smokers now get through 60 per cent more cigarettes a day than a generation ago, which makes them the heaviest female smokers in the world.[4]

Not only do women smoke more heavily than their counterparts of 25 years ago—they are also much younger. There is now

11

evidence that in some countries the proportion of young girls who smoke has overtaken that of boys. In 1979—for the first time in the history of the cigarette—there were more American teenage girls who smoked than there were boys. Nearly four in every ten teenage girls are now smoking 20 cigarettes a day.[5] In Britain, girls giving up are almost matched by the increasing numbers of girls starting to smoke. Ten years ago, teenage boys smoked much more heavily than girls, but today are slowing down while girls smoke as heavily as the boys.[6] We can, perhaps, get a clue about possible future trends from what has already happened in Sweden. There, as long ago as 1971, *more* 15-year-old girls smoked than boys of the same age.

These smoking patterns are not peculiar to Britain and America, and Table I (below) shows that the pattern is similar for most of Europe and the developed world.

The proportion of women smokers is either rising or stable in 12 of the 16 countries shown in the table, whilst it is *falling* among men in as many countries. Thus, with minor exceptions such as the USA, the picture is the same: everywhere, smoking is increasing in women and declining in men. In Norway, there were signs of a slight decline among women between 1974 and 1977, but it has now levelled off.[17] In the USA there has been a five per cent drop between 1964 and 1979,[18] but the overall pattern is not markedly different from elsewhere; there has been far more substantial decline among men.

Not Only a Question of Sex

The successful ex-smoker is male, married, a college graduate, has three or four children, and has smoked for less than ten years.[19-21] He is someone 'whose image is associated with worldly success'.[22] Not only is he a family man, he is also likely to have a wife who disapproves of his smoking and who supports him in his efforts to stop. He is a man who has confidence in himself, and his ability to stop.[23,24] On the other hand, it seems that many of the factors which combine to produce a successful male ex-smoker have precisely the *opposite* effect in women. Marriage and parenthood for a woman mean she is *less* likely to have successfully stopped smoking.[25] And for a woman, a disapproving husband or child makes it harder and not easier to stop.[26]

Most ex-smokers are middle-class professionals (who are largely male)—the doctors, lawyers and university teachers—

Table I: Smoking Trends in the Developed World[7-16]

COUNTRY	YEAR	DIRECTION OF SMOKING TREND	
		FEMALE	MALE
Australia	1975	↑	↓
Austria	1972	↑	↔
Belgium	1979	↓	↓
Canada	1977	↔	↓
Denmark	1972	↑	↑
Finland	1977	↔	↓
France	1977	↓	↓
W. Germany	1973	↑	↓
Italy	1973	↑	↑
Netherlands	1972	↔	↓
New Zealand	1976	↑	↓
Norway	1980	↔	↓
Sweden	1977	↑	↓
Switzerland	1975	↑	↑
United Kingdom	1975	↔	↓
USA	1979	small ↓	↓

Key: ↑ = proportion of smokers rising
  ↓ = proportion of smokers falling
  ↔ = proportion of smokers remains steady

13

while the highest proportions of smokers are found among blacks, the low paid, and those who have had little educational opportunity.[27–29] In the USA, there is a racial *and* a sexual hierarchy among ex-smokers. White women have lower rates of stopping than white men, but higher than black men and higher still than black women.[30] In 1978, black men had the highest smoking rates of all in the US.[31] Roughly equal proportions of black and white American women now smoke (30 per cent), but black women smoke more dangerously, with nearly one in five still on non-filter cigarettes.[32]

Smoking patterns, thus, also reflect the politics of a class society. Irrespective of whether you are male or female, the lower your status, income and educational achievements, the more likely you are to smoke. But class alone cannot explain smoking trends in women: women *within every social group* have lower rates of stopping than do men. Thus, women's smoking patterns reflect under-privilege of a different kind: that of sex. *Smoking rates among women are high at both ends of the social scale.* So far, the USA, Canada and France are the only countries where researchers have studied the factors in women's own lives—rather than those of their husbands—that affect their smoking habits. Taking the USA, we see that, in 1979, 42 per cent of women managers and administrators smoked compared with only 37 per cent of their male 'white collar' counterparts. Women managers, although at the upper end of the social scale, smoke more than almost any other group of women, including 'blue collar' workers who have traditionally had high smoking rates. These women managers are joined by heavy-smoking service workers at the other end of the social scale.[33] It seems that women with high incomes and prestigious jobs tend to smoke *alongside* women with low-paid, low-status jobs. Why should this be?

Women Find it Harder to Stop Smoking than Men

Women are as aware of the risks of smoking as men, and they certainly try to stop smoking as often or more often than men.[34–36] But they have lower success rates *in every occupational and age group*—except the very young, where there are no real differences between the sexes.[37]

As the 1980 US Surgeon-General's report on women and smoking put it:

Across all treatments, women have more difficulty giving up smoking than men. No studies have been reported in which women do significantly better than men. Several of the larger studies show higher abstinence rates by men.

A month's monitoring of hundreds of requests for help at the ASH (Action on Smoking & Health) office showed that up to three-quarters came from women. This trend has been confirmed by researchers in Oxford monitoring an offer of help to stop smoking, broadcast by the TV programme *Reports Action*. Of the 425,000 people who responded, *seven out of ten* were women.[38] I further confirmed the trend in a survey of the 24 regular smokers' clinics run by local health authorities. Of the 21 who replied to my questionnaire, two-thirds reported that the majority of their clients were women and a similar proportion observed that the women found it harder to stop than the men.

Further confirmatory evidence comes from wide-scale national surveys conducted in several countries, which show that women are only about half as successful as men at stopping smoking and that this finding applies across most age and social groups. Finally, monitored trials that test specific methods of helping smokers to stop, which can be used to compare groups of men and women *all* highly motivated to give up, show that men are up to twice as successful as women at stopping—irrespective of the method used.[39] Moreover, even women who do stop seem to return to cigarettes more rapidly than do men who have undergone the same course. In one Canadian study in which nearly 500 people tried to stop smoking with the help of a four-week course, 60 per cent of the men and 55 per cent of the women were off cigarettes at the end of the course. After three months, 50 per cent of the men had continued to resist smoking, but there was a steeper decline in the number of women who were able to do likewise. After a year, 34 per cent of the men had become 'fully-fledged' ex-smokers, compared with only 20 per cent of the women.[40]

The Price Women are Paying Worldwide

In 1977, more than 8,500 British women died of lung cancer.[41-43] Which means that one women dies of lung cancer every hour of the day, every day of the week, to maintain Britain in its unenviable third position in the Women's World Lung Cancer

League (see Table II below). Although American women rank lower—ninth—in the league, the American Cancer Society estimated that more than seventy American women would die of lung cancer each day in 1980.[44] British women owe their higher lung-cancer rates not only to their higher smoking rates, but also to lower levels of affluence than in the USA. Instead of reducing overall smoking rates, relative poverty has, ironically, encouraged British women (and men) to smoke more dangerously than their American contemporaries. British women—presumably after their money's worth—smoke their way further down each cigarette, where the concentration of the cancer-producing tar is highest. American women, on the other hand, who have been able to afford to throw away longer cigarette stubs, have unwittingly limited their lung-cancer toll.

Table II: The Women's World Lung Cancer League: The Top Twenty[45]

LEAGUE POSITION	COUNTRY	LUNG CANCER DEATH RATE/100,000 (AGED 45+)
1	Hong Kong	95
2	Cuba	73
3	UK	62
4	Singapore	59
5	Ireland	53
6	Iceland	51
7	Denmark	43
8	New Zealand	41
9	USA	40
10	Hungary	36
11	Canada	34
12	Luxembourg	34
13	Israel	33
14	Australia	29
15	Venezuela	29
16	Argentina	28
17	Costa Rica	28
18	Puerto Rico	28
19	Bulgaria	27
20	Taiwan	27

Hong Kong women lead the World Lung Cancer League, and Singapore women are not far behind with lung-cancer rates almost as high as the UK. It is not clear why this should be so, and whether it relates to the type of smoking material used or to other factors. Neither the World Health Organisation nor I have, so far, been able to trace a single published national survey of smoking rates among either Hong Kong or Singapore women. Indeed, in a recent study in Hong Kong, the authors were forced to admit that they did not know why lung-cancer rates were high among female non-smokers as well as smokers.[46] The latest evidence, however, suggests that they may be due to long-term exposure to cigarette smoke from their husbands who tend to smoke heavily.[47]

Although lung cancer is the most clear-cut example of an illness caused by smoking, cigarettes are also a major cause of coronary heart disease in which the arteries feeding the heart muscle become blocked—often causing a heart attack. In numerical terms, coronary heart disease is the number-one killer of both women *and* men in the western world. In 1979, more than 65,000 women in England and Wales died of coronary heart disease, which claims *more women than all forms of cancer combined.*[48] Although smoking is not the only cause of heart disease, and dietary and other factors are also of key importance, the woman who smokes twenty cigarettes a day is twice as likely to die of a heart attack as her non-smoking contemporaries—*irrespective* of any other risk factors.[49] Moreover, women who smoke and take the oral contraceptive pill face the risk of heart disease due to the pill itself, *multiplied* by that of smoking.[50] A woman who takes the pill and smokes 25 cigarettes a day is forty times more likely to have a heart attack than a woman who neither smokes nor takes the pill.[51] Women face a similar compounded risk of a particular kind of brain haemorrhage—known as a sub-arachnoid haemorrhage—if they take the pill and smoke as well.[52]

Smoking is also the main cause of chronic bronchitis and emphysema—two disabling and ultimately fatal chest diseases (see Valerie's account on pages 9–10). Although milder cigarettes, cleaner air and improved medical treatment have contributed to the steady decline of these illnesses in both men and women, they still kill more British women than the total number of people killed on the roads.[53]

3. Tomorrow's Casualties

So cigarettes are already the biggest single cause of premature death and ill-health in both men and women in the western world, and are a growing cause for concern in less affluent countries. At the moment, women in a more developed country such as Britain or the US live roughly seven years longer than men. Researchers have calculated that between one-third and one-half of this difference in life-expectancy can be attributed to women's lower smoking rates.[1] If smoking rates continue to go down in men, and women don't stop, that gap in life-expectancy could be closed during the next century.

Next Century's Cigarette Victims

Although three to four times as many men as women in more developed countries die of lung cancer, the peak of the epidemic in men is over. The female peak is yet to come. Lower-tar cigarettes will probably ensure that the high point for women will never be as high as that for men. Yet, in just one generation, lung-cancer rates have increased four-fold among American women[2] and predictions are that by 1983, lung-cancer rates in American women will have overtaken those for breast cancer—which killed 35,000 American women in 1979.[3]

In Britain, there are the first signs of lung cancer levelling off in men, but the recent rise in the female lung-cancer rate shows every sign of continuing. Between 1969 and 1978, lung-cancer rates increased by more than fifty per cent among women, but by only eight per cent in men.[4] By next century, nearly as many younger and middle-aged women may die of lung cancer as their male contemporaries and, if present trends continue, some researchers predict that women could even overtake men in their lung-cancer rates in fifty years' time.[5] Although it is unlikely that women will actually overtake men, predictions from current figures suggest that, by the year 2010, their death rate from lung cancer will

18

exceed that from breast cancer—which currently kills 12,000 women a year.[6]

Patterns of coronary heart disease in women show a similar upward trend—in Britain at least. Because the factors shaping trends in heart disease are much more complicated than those affecting lung cancer, and because research on heart disease in women is inadequate, it is not easy to sketch the future. But US trends show a recent decline in both men and women. It is difficult to say whether this will continue in the long-term. Certainly, many women now face new risks which could adversely influence their prospects. First, increasing numbers of women are now going out to work and, as a result, smoking more than ever before. For the first time, women are seriously competing with men for jobs, and the aggressiveness and competitiveness which are prerequisites for success in a male world seem to be implicated in heart disease in women[7] as well as in men.[8]

Second, there are ten million women throughout the world who take the contraceptive pill[9] and large numbers who also smoke. As the pill continues to be heavily promoted in the third world, we can expect more young women, both in the west and elsewhere, to die of coronary heart disease in the coming decades. Increasing numbers of middle-class women have stopped taking the pill and the majority now taking it are working-class women with high smoking rates. Against the depressing picture so far, it does seem certain that there will be a further welcome decline in the death rate from chronic bronchitis and emphysema. But they will continue to cause substantial ill-health and disability in Britain, both in men and women—especially those who smoke as well as living in an industrially-polluted part of the country.

Which Women?

If smoking patterns remain unchanged, the cigarette will claim most of its victims from three main groups of women. First are the under-paid and under-privileged in the more developed countries. Cigarettes are already claiming both the women and the men who can least afford to smoke but who are, nevertheless, among today's heaviest smokers. They will continue to be the prime casualties next century. Among this group of women are the doubly under-privileged—those who are discriminated against on the grounds of both race and sex. Women from minority ethnic groups are often poor and almost always poorer than their white

19

equivalents. Their jobs are often the lowest paid and their living conditions the least satisfactory. It is hardly surprising, therefore, that black American women have responded far more slowly to pleas to stop smoking than their white counterparts.[10] And it can be no coincidence that Maori women in New Zealand and coloured women in South Africa have the highest smoking rates— often higher than those of most men—of all women in the more developed world.[11,12] The inevitable consequences of this are evident in the increasing lung cancer rates among black women, which are already higher than for white women.[13] Today's so-called independent career women will be the second group to succumb to the cigarette. Hailed by the advertisers as their most lucrative target since the last war (see chapter 9), these women will certainly join next century's casualties. Although still a small group today, it could grow if increasing numbers of women take up careers.

The Third World—A Market Waiting to be Tapped

Men and women from third-world countries will undoubtedly swell the casualty statistics most. The tobacco trade press has described them as 'potentially lucrative' and 'receptive' new markets.[14] All the big tobacco companies have major interests in less developed countries. British American Tobacco alone— the world's largest tobacco company—sells 300 different brands in 180 countries while Philip Morris—makers of the world's best-selling cigarette, Marlboro—have a growing third-world trade which is expanding at a rate of 18 per cent a year.[15] It makes good sense for a tobacco company to invest heavily in the third world. Apart from women, the rest of the cigarette-market has apparently reached saturation in most western countries. Thus, soaring population growth in the South American, African and Asian continents makes the potential for expansion enormous, with hardly any controls on tobacco advertising, and little awareness— as yet—of health hazards.

Tobacco companies have helped to persuade farming families —and governments—to grow tobacco instead of food. And projections for 1980 show that the companies' tactics are paying off. They don't expect overall smoking rates in Europe and America to increase much, but look forward to sales going up by as much as a third in Africa, and a quarter in Latin America and Asia.[16] Increasing contact between the west and The People's Republic of

20

China has also enabled the tobacco companies to explore the potential of this new market representing a quarter of the world's people.[17] To third-world people, cigarette smoking is synonymous with opulence, success and, above all, modernisation. Thus, the growing numbers of third-world smokers—both men and women—are a tribute to the power of cigarette advertising which sells the image of 'the very special taste of success' in the African version of State Express 555 cigarettes, or the Middle Eastern variety which has 'a little more style than the rest'.

The battle to win third-world women over to cigarettes is being fought between the cigarette companies and the forces of religious and cultural control. The tobacco companies' access to women depends largely on existing cultural beliefs determining the status of women in any given community. Ironically, the lower a woman's status, the greater her protection from the commercial assaults. But at a time of rapid change in the role of women in many societies, even yashmaks are no armour against the cigarette.

Three Potential Recipes for Ill-Health

In traditional Arab and Asian communities, cigarette smoking is still rare. To risk smoking—especially in public—is to be labelled a 'fallen woman'. Yet, even these barriers are beginning to fall. High-class middle-eastern ladies have begun to experiment with cigarettes. One shocked observer in Kuwait reported that 'for the first time recently, I saw Arab women, often in traditional dress, smoking cigarettes in front of their menfolk without any apparent inhibition'. Another observer in Morocco described how increasing numbers of female students were not only wearing western clothes, but were smoking cigarettes. Traditional forms of smoking already predominate in India and elsewhere although the commercial cigarette is encroaching in the cities. In rural parts of India, tobacco chewing and reverse chutta smoking—which involves smoking locally-grown cheroots with the burning end inside the mouth—are common practices in women, and the preliminary research shows that rates of cancer of the mouth—believed to be caused by reverse chutta smoking—are high among these women.[18] Though taboos shield Moslem women from smoking, Hindu and Christian women do not face this constraint and seem likely to emulate their menfolk.

In countries such as Japan, there is an uneasy alliance between two cultures. On the one hand, there is the traditional oriental community in which women play a very subordinate role and, on the other, the increasing influence of the west which has brought turbulence and change to the lives of many Japanese women. The view that women who smoke are either prostitutes or drop-outs is balanced against the increasingly common sight of the 'liberated woman' who smokes casually in the fashionable tea-shops of Japan's major cities. The confusing signs of the times are reflected in Japanese women's smoking patterns. Smoking rates are low—less than one in ten are smokers—among older women who, presumably, have been strongly influenced by past traditions. By contrast, smoking is now rising among women under thirty.[19]

Under the Influence: Africa and Latin America

It seems that the cigarette is also making its mark in Africa. In Nigeria, where only just over one per cent of all women smoke, there is evidence of the encroachment of smoking from research in the medical schools where twenty per cent of the female students now smoke.[20] The tobacco companies are losing no time in furnishing the right cigarette images for women as well as men. Cigarettes such as Embassy Menthol and Embassy Sweet Menthol, with enticing advertisements showing women smoking, are becoming familiar on Kenyan billboards. They have, according to recent research, 'potential' within the women's market.[21] But the most depressing story by far comes from Latin America.

Despite an increasingly affluent veneer, most South American cities are characterised by a teeming populace, stark poverty and overcrowding. Indeed, cigarettes have been so effectively equated with dreams of western affluence that the proportion of Uruguayan women who smoke is now *higher* than for American women as a whole. Thirty-two per cent of women in Caracas now smoke, compared with twenty-eight per cent of all American women, and this gap is likely to increase in coming years. In cities such as Santiago, La Plata, Sao Paulo and Bogota, the proportion of women who smoke is comparable with smoking rates for women in Europe[22] and in some cases exceeds it. Venezuelan women are now fifteenth in the Women's Lung Cancer League[23] and it is still early days there. Latin-American women are racing to the grave at almost the same pace as men.

4. Why Women Smoke—The Experts' View

Most researchers agree that the factors which prompt a child to try cigarettes are quite distinct from those which compel an adult to continue smoking. They also agree that the reasons a child starts to smoke are largely social. We know that most children have their first cigarette when they are very young—often less than 10.[1] And contrary to the popular view that children secretly puff on their first cigarette in the shed at the bottom of the garden, research shows that children usually accept their first cigarette from a member of the family—a sister, brother, or even a parent.[2] It may seem a truism, but non-smoking parents tend to produce non-smoking children. Young children are strongly influenced by the models their parents and other members of the family present. It is hardly surprising that research confirms boys tend to copy smoking fathers and brothers, and girls their mothers and sisters.[3] It is easy to see how a vicious circle can rapidly establish itself: the poorer the parents, and the less well-educated they are, the more likely they—and therefore their children—are to smoke.

As a child gets older, influences outside the home such as school and friends become more important. Children who smoke tend to have smoking friends and there is also evidence that smoking teachers have more smoking pupils than non-smoking teachers.[4,5] Although few researchers have tried to assess the importance of cigarette advertising in encouraging older children to copy the heroes and heroines of the ads, there is evidence from Canada that teenage boys who smoke tend to choose cigarettes with a 'macho' image, while girls choose the more 'feminine' sophisticated brands.[6]

While broadly agreeing on what prompts girls and boys to start smoking, researchers are still baffled by what drives people to continue. Indeed the theories offered often tell us as much about the vested interests of a particular researcher as they do about smokers. Psychologists, for instance, are expected to propose psychological theories while those in pharmacology or addiction research departments predictably offer physiological theories on smoking.

Do Women Smoke for Nicotine?

There are many who believe that chemistry can explain why people continue to smoke. Ronda is 60 and has been smoking for 25 years. She is convinced that she is 'an addict who cannot get off the hook'. Her first husband died when she was 35 leaving her to cope with three young children, and her second husband was an alcoholic who 'made life intolerable for all of us'. Ronda is now lonely, depressed, and in permanent pain due to a nerve injury in her leg.

Despite the many emotional and social reasons Ronda could choose to explain her smoking, she is convinced that she is 'chemically addicted to it [tobacco]. I know I am weak-willed. I could have taken up the "bottle" when my husband died but I took up nicotine instead.' Ronda is not alone in her belief that she is addicted to nicotine. Every woman who discussed her smoking problem with me was convinced she was 'hooked' on nicotine.

But is nicotine addictive? According to the Royal College of Physicians' latest report, *Smoking* or *Health*, 'Tobacco smoking is a form of drug dependence different from, but no less strong than that of other addictive drugs.' The report concludes that 'most smokers continue to indulge in the habit because they are addicted to nicotine.'[7] But is there good reason to believe that nicotine alone is responsible for dependence on cigarettes? Some of the evidence does indeed point to nicotine causing physical addiction. First, nicotine reaches and affects the brain in only seven seconds. Second, nicotine does seem to be responsible for the sensations smokers attribute to cigarettes, stimulation on the one hand, and sedation on the other. Animal experiments have shown that in small doses, nicotine acts as a stimulant, and in bigger doses it can tranquillise.[8] Biochemical experiments have shown, too, that nicotine can cause the release of chemical transmitters in the brain which could be responsible for the observed effects[9] and experiments in human subjects suggest it aids concentration and improves long-term memory and performance of simple tasks.[10]

But if we assumed that tobacco's nicotine content alone was responsible for cigarette addiction, we would expect people to smoke primarily to maintain nicotine blood levels. It follows that smokers who switched from a higher to a lower nicotine cigarette

24

brand would need to compensate for the reduction in nicotine by smoking more or inhaling more. Some researchers claim they do; others say that no such compensation takes place. Experiments in which smokers boost their nicotine levels by chewing nicotine-containing gum have shown that they do reduce the amount they smoke.[11] More recent experiments in which smokers were switched (without knowing) to higher or lower nicotine cigarette brands also showed they seemed to compensate by smoking (and inhaling) less or more respectively.[12] But low nicotine cigarettes are also low in tar which is a key determinant of taste, so that it is not clear whether smokers in these experiments are compensating for taste or for nicotine. There was also evidence that the compensation only occurred in the short term: two weeks after a switch to a lower nicotine brand, smokers returned to their previous smoking pattern.[13] Even more confusingly, other recent research suggests there is no compensation at all and that smokers given injections of nicotine to 'supplement' their smoking do not adjust their smoking habits in any way.[14]

By far the most important criteria for establishing whether a drug is physically addictive are the phenomena of 'tolerance' and 'withdrawal syndrome' which are characteristic of narcotic drugs such as barbiturates and opiates (morphine-like drugs). 'Tolerance' means that as drug use continues, the drug-taker becomes 'dependent' and needs more and more of the drug to achieve the desired effect. The 'withdrawal syndrome', by contrast, results from sudden stoppage of the drug supply; the nerves affected by the drug become overactive during a possibly unpleasant but short re-adaptation period.

Nicotine fits some, but not all of the criteria for physical dependence. Smokers who experiment with the occasional cigarette rapidly begin to tolerate the nausea and headiness that smoking causes. They soon find themselves smoking more and more—needing to smoke every day (only 2 per cent of all smokers remain truly occasional smokers). Yet they don't keep on stepping up the 'dose' of nicotine and usually settle for between 10 and 25 cigarettes a day. Indeed the amount smoked seems as much a reflection of economic and social pressures as internal chemical forces. When people try to stop smoking they may well experience unpleasant 'withdrawal symptoms' (see chapter 18) but, unlike narcotic drug addicts who stop, many don't.

The evidence is incomplete and even conflicting. It therefore seems premature to single out nicotine as the addictive culprit especially as we now know that tolerance can develop to carbon monoxide, tar, acetone and phenol—to mention but four of the remaining 1,000 components of tobacco smoke.[15] Scientists often cite the low success rate for stopping smoking—about a quarter are able to stop even though up to 90 per cent want to stop—as further evidence of the physical origin of cigarette dependence.[16,17] Yet the difficulty many smokers experience in stopping could also be psychological or social in origin. Indeed when the motivation to stop is very high, such as an increase in tax on cigarettes or in smokers who have had a heart attack, the success rate for stopping can more than double.[18] Perhaps the strongest challenge to the idea of straightforward nicotine addiction is the simple observation that social status is a more important determinant of who smokes and who stops (see chapter 2) than either psychological *or* physiological makeup. To invoke nicotine dependence to explain why doctors have found it easier to give up than labourers, and indeed why women find it harder to stop smoking than men, you would have to support the unlikely proposition that there is something about being a doctor (or a man) that confers physiological resistance to the addictive pull of tobacco.

Is There a Smoker's Personality?

Alongside theories of nicotine addiction, researchers also explored the idea of the 'smoker's personality'. In the early days of research, psychologists thought smokers might be slightly 'crazy', but could not find any evidence to support this.[19] So they insisted on pursuing the idea that specific personality traits could explain why people were 'prone' to smoking. This began the search for a 'smoker's personality'. Thousands of smokers (and non-smokers) completed questionnaires ostensibly testing 'anxiety levels', 'extroversion' and 'introversion' levels, and that elusive idea of 'personality' itself. Psychologists concluded that smokers were more 'extroverted' than non-smokers. They were the risk-takers, were more sociable, impulsive, and carefree than non-smokers. About half the published studies made further claims that women smokers were more 'neurotic' than both non-smokers and male smokers.[20] The other half found no differences between male and female smoker 'neurosis' levels.

How important are these supposed differences? Neuroticism and extroversion account for about 1 per cent and 3 per cent respectively of the differences between smokers and non-smokers.[21] Which leaves more than 95 per cent of the differences unexplained! To interpret smoking patterns in personality terms alone, you would have to postulate that smokers who have stopped—some 8 million Britons and 30 million Americans—have undergone a personality change. The sweeping generalisations resulting from these tests have proved of little practical value. Even if it were possible satisfactorily to prove that women smokers are more neurotic than men, it would tell us little about the specific anxieties and stresses in women's lives that may prompt them to smoke.

Smoker Types

Following the unsuccessful search for the 'smoker's personality', psychologists began to widen the boundaries imposed by personality tests and concentrated on isolating what they called 'smoking types'. Although they still drew heavily on previous personality research, there was a difference in emphasis. They moved away from defining the smoker by personality alone, and acknowledged, for the first time, that environment could contribute to the need to smoke. In 1965, an American psychologist, Sylvan Tomkins, proposed four basic types of smoking:[22]

Positive affect smoking: This takes place when the smoker feels relaxed or bored and uses smoking for a boost.
Sedative (negative affect) smoking: This occurs when the smoker feels uncomfortable or ill-at-ease. The smoker uses sedative smoking to reduce and thus to cope with negative feelings. The complete sedative smoker, says Tomkins, 'avoids a confrontation with the source of suffering, relying solely on smoking to reduce negative affect.'
Habitual smoking: This occurs under more emotionally neutral circumstances when the smoker appears to get little out of smoking and is often oblivious to the fact of smoking.
Addictive smoking: This is a combination of the first two types.

Daniel Horn, Director of the former US National Clearing House on Smoking and Health, along with his colleagues, further expanded Tomkins' four types by dividing 'positive affect smoking' into stimulation smoking, relaxation smoking, and manipulation smoking—those who enjoy handling cigarettes.

27

They compiled a questionnaire to divide smokers into the six smoking types. In a study of more than 2,000 people[23] the most striking difference they found between male and female smokers was that the women tended to smoke much more to reduce their negative feelings than the men who, in turn, were more likely to indulge in habitual smoking. The women smoked more when they felt 'uncomfortable or upset about something' or when they were 'angry, ashamed or embarrassed about something' or when they wanted to 'take their mind off cares and worries'. This difference in the circumstances under which men and women smoke was highlighted in more recent research in which 57 male and female undergraduates watched a horror film, containing brutal torture scenes, and a comedy film. The researchers found that nearly three-quarters of the women smoked during the horror film compared with only one-third of the men, yet none of the women and most of the men smoked during the comedy film. They concluded that the women smoked mainly to 'reduce negative affect' in the horror film while most men seemed to have little need for sedative smoking. By contrast, the men seemed to smoke 'for positive affect' during the comedy film.[24]

Other psychologists have attempted to refine and adjust the typology tests using slightly different criteria. Michael Russell, a psychiatrist at the Addiction Research Unit in London, tried to combine both psychological and social factors in a typology scale of seven types of smoking, adding 'psychosocial smoking' to the list. Russell found women were much more likely than men to engage in what he called 'sedative smoking' whereas men tended to prefer 'stimulation' or 'manipulation' smoking.[25] Community physician Walter Fee, who conducted smoker typology tests on all smokers attending his smokers' clinic in Dundee, Scotland, confirmed these differences. Only one-quarter of the men attending the clinic were 'sedative' smokers, compared with nearly half the women. The men, concluded Fee, 'appeared to smoke more for pleasure than the women'. He also noticed that the proportion of sedative smokers attending the clinic had increased dramatically between 1970 and 1974, as had the proportion of women attending over the same period.[26]

Thus smoker typology tests give us an important insight into why smoking patterns in men and women are different. They tell us that women often feel the need to smoke under different circumstances than men. But the typology tests also suffer some of

28

the same weaknesses as personality tests in that they measure only a few, narrowly defined aspects of the problem. The smoker types are defined as being distinct from one another, which limits their practical use, because smokers themselves often fall into several types. So although they are useful in telling us that women tend to use cigarettes to cope with their anger and frustrations more than men do, they do not tell us *why*.

5. Why Do Women Smoke?

It is clear from the research so far that neither nicotine addiction nor smoker typology can adequately explain why people smoke. We can, however, gain further insight into the problem by looking more closely at how women themselves understand their need to smoke—an avenue usually avoided by the experts.

Learning to Smoke

Tanya is a 30-year-old housewife, and smokes 20 cigarettes a day. She remembers her first cigarette very well: 'I started when I was 12. My father had remarried, and although my step-sister was only a year older than me, she seemed so much more mature in her dress and her ways. My step-mother let her smoke, and she took the mickey out of me because I couldn't smoke properly. I got my own back by stealing her cigarettes and going into the bedroom to practise smoking until I could do it without looking stupid.'

Smoking is one of the forbidden fruits of adulthood. It seems to be associated with things only grown-ups do. Catherine started smoking when she was 18—just before her 'A' level exams—partly because she associated smoking with 'calming the nerves and relieving anxiety' and partly because 'it made me feel that I had, in some way, graduated to adulthood; I felt quite proud of myself.'

Smoking also appeals to a child's sense of curiosity. The girl who tries on her mother's lipstick and clothes when she is out may find her cigarettes lying around and try them too. Nancy had her first cigarette just before appearing on stage when she was 18:

'There was no pressure from anyone to do so . . . I had an almost disinterested curiosity in cigarettes. I wanted to know if what they said about cigarettes was true. I was trying to discover if smoking really did help one overcome anxiety at such times.'

Although Tanya's early experiences with cigarettes were anything but pleasant, she was determined to tread the path to adulthood: 'I even remember the brand of the first packet of cigarettes I bought, because they had such a bloody horrible taste. I didn't enjoy them; they made me feel sick. But I felt incredibly grown-up buying them. They made me feel that I was a big girl.'

Claudia, a 37-year-old secretary, started smoking when she was 11: 'I remember being bored one night and finding my mother's cigarettes lying around. I tried one because I wanted to mimic what I had always seen her do. Smoking was always very important for her, and I felt somehow closer to mum by copying her. It was always curiously reassuring to see her light a cigarette.'

Smoking is also a friendly thing to do. It is a way of saying 'Hello, I like you'—especially to boys. Most girls who smoke also have friends who smoke and the cigarette is a way of making those friendships special. It is a means of identifying with a special group and feeling part of it. Susie is in her last year at school. She started smoking two years ago. For Susie it was a conscious decision—a way of joining the local elite: 'My image at school was that I was too good. I found that frustrating because I felt it didn't show me up for the little rebel I thought I really was. When I started smoking, people began to be nicer to me—especially those who had laughed at me before. I used to skulk off with them every break and lunch hour for that fag we all so desperately needed.'

Helen, who is 21, started smoking at 13. She saw smoking as a means of narrowing the gap between herself and her fellow students whom she saw as intellectually less able: 'I started primarily because it was forbidden, and therefore quite exciting for a couple of us to smoke behind the back of authority. I began to inhale and smoke more heavily at the age of fifteen. I think it was an attempt to prove to contemporaries lower down the "intelligence ranks" at school that the snobs (such as myself) could smoke just as well as everyone else. Meeting in the school lavatories for a surreptitious smoke helped to break down the unpleasant intellectual barriers between us at the time. It helped to provide some common ground between us.'

Kathy started smoking a year ago: 'The first time I smoked a whole cigarette was when I was with a boyfriend who was older than me. There were two other boys there, one of whom offered me a cigarette. Everybody took one—including me. I felt that it somehow brought me closer to them and also defined me as a person rather than a silly girl. The initial offering and sharing of cigarettes, to me, forms an immediate social bond.'

What Keeps Women Smoking?

We could define smokers, much as the researchers have done—in general terms. Thus it is true to say that every smoker fits somewhere in a spectrum marked, at one extreme, by those who have no intention of stopping and those, at the other end, who would dearly love to stop, but can't. But the teenage girl who defiantly refuses to stop smoking may be transformed in a few years into a woman who desperately wants to stop.

Women Smokers' Defences

In the face of mounting evidence on the hazards of smoking, most smokers have learned to defend their habit. Many of the defences are obvious rationalisations, but some are explanations which cannot be brushed aside so easily.

'*I'm only a moderate smoker.*' This is a classically female defence, and many women sincerely believe it, despite smoking nearly as heavily as men. Much more pervasive, however, is the assumption that '*It's much more likely to affect a man.*' Although increasing numbers of women are becoming ill through cigarettes, it is not yet as common to see women suffering the effects of lung cancer or a heart attack as it is to see men, many of whom have been moved to stop in recent years by the illness of a contemporary.

'*I accept what they say about smoking, but the warnings really have no relevance to my life.*' Few women (or men) would be prepared to give public voice to this subconscious reason, probably one of the most potent. Health reports issue warnings that we lose five-and-a-half minutes of our life each time we smoke a cigarette, but how much priority does desire for a long life get in the lives of most ordinary men and women? The prospect of losing ten years of life may not be uppermost in the mind of a woman factory-worker who alternates day and night shifts with her husband to make ends meet.

'*I smoke because I enjoy it.*' Although my own surveys

31

indicate that men smoke out of a sense of enjoyment more often than do women, this is also an important woman smoker's defence. But enjoyment is rarely the only reason a woman smokes, and is certainly never the reason for starting. The cigarette with a drink or after a meal is often the most enjoyable and the most satisfying, but other motives may be involved. It may be a device to stop eating or to help the smoker feel more at ease.

Suppressing the Unacceptable

Although most smokers rationalise their smoking to some extent, we must look more deeply into the kinds of lives women lead if we are to understand why a woman's need to smoke is different from a man's.

Annie is 28 and smokes 20 cigarettes a day. When she feels bored or 'under stress' she smokes an extra ten. 'I couldn't contemplate stopping', says Annie, 'because my biggest fear would be having nothing to rely on in a stressful or frightening situation.' Like Annie, Pauline also smokes at emotional high-points in the day: 'Cigarettes are a comfort and a cover-up for the many fears and embarrassments I encounter in my life. The moment I feel under any kind of stress, my first thought is to resort to smoking.'

Pauline and Annie, like so many women and some men, use their smoking as a safety valve, an alternative to letting off steam. They smoke not to accompany expressions of frustration or anxiety, but *instead of expressing these feelings*. As some researchers have said, women smoke to 'reduce negative affect'. Why? Claudia soon began to recognise the motives behind her smoking. She smoked heavily in all highly-charged emotional circumstances: 'My cigarettes were a barometer of how I felt. If I was tense, I smoked more cigarettes. If I wasn't sleeping, I smoked more cigarettes. There was a predictable consistency in my self-destructive behaviour. If I was feeling relaxed and good in relation to myself, I would probably cut down on the number of cigarettes I smoked. It all seemed to hinge on how I viewed myself. I increased the amount I smoked to 60 a day after a very unhappy relationship with a man. After that point in my life, whenever I hit any kind of distress I would deal with it with a cigarette.'

As a secretary, Claudia often felt powerless and frustrated at work: 'If you watched me with a cigarette, you could see that I usually smoked when I was feeling anxious or distressed. I always found it difficult to express my anger and anxieties. Cigarettes were important to me because they helped to suppress a lot of these feelings. They were the only outside evidence of my feelings I was able to tolerate.'

Aileen is a 57-year-old cook who smoked up to 40 cigarettes a day before her heart operation. She now smokes between 15 and 20 a day. She and her husband are separated. When her six children were young, Aileen had neither the time nor money to smoke much. The number she smoked shot up about five years ago as things deteriorated between her and her husband.

'What upset me most was knowing that he'd made a right fool of me all these years. When I was sitting at home looking after the children, he was out enjoying himself or working overseas. And I'd sit at home thinking and thinking about how I'd been left to bring the family up on my own. And, of course, I'd smoke cigarette after cigarette to help calm me down a bit. I think my smoking went sky-high then because it was such a difficult period in my life. We couldn't afford a baby-sitter until six years ago. So I had no choice but to stay in. I had to wait until the eldest was 18 and a capable baby-sitter before I could allow myself to go out to the pictures.

'Even when the children were old enough for us to be able to start going out together again, he still went off with his cronies. And he liked his drink too much. He came home drunk no end of times. When he started ranting, I used to be scared he might kill the kids. I remember one time when he hadn't been home all week-end, I'd been doing some washing—using the spin-drier. Suddenly everything in it seemed to go red. He'd hit me in the mouth, and I'd bled into the machine. I had to have three teeth out, and I've still got a loose one. I should have left him years ago, but I couldn't because of the kids. We've now been separated for three years, but I only get £1 through the separation order. I'm glad he's left, because he's still unemployed and claiming sickness benefit, but it's been hard to make the money stretch far enough.'

Aileen would love to stop smoking and has every health incentive to do so. But, like many other women, she needs her cigarettes to maintain her calm.

Women have a bigger emotional investment in smoking than men. Cigarettes represent one of the few ways of uncorking those feelings that society teaches them to suppress. Mrs X, who is 64 and smokes 20 cigarettes a day, puts it another way: 'Cigarette smoking not so much calms the nerves as dulls the sensibilities so that I, at least, do not care so much that I am frustrated.' Men do not, of course, escape similar frustrations, but there are more channels through which they can express these pent-up emotions. Society may not like a drunken man, but it approves even less of a drunken woman. Aggressive behaviour—whether desirable or not—is always an easier avenue for release of tension for men. This does not necessarily mean that women are innately less aggressive than men, but rather that women are *expected* to be so. Despite living in an age of 'sexual liberation', sexual freedom does not apply equally for men and women. Even exercise—a seemingly innocuous outlet—is still a more acceptable activity for men than for women.

Not only do women smoke to keep their emotions in check, many dare not stop for fear of what may happen if they can't prevent their emotions from leaking out. Will her boss sack her if she answers him back next time instead of having a cigarette? Will her husband leave her if she gets fed up and irritable about holding down a job as well as running a home? Will her children stop loving her if she turns from the loving mother into a momentarily angry woman?

Mrs S. is 46 and smokes 20 cigarettes a day. She admits to using her cigarettes as a safety valve. She has smoked a lot more since having a hysterectomy which left her feeling 'forlorn and run down'. Her cigarettes were a comfort to her, a way of dealing with being depressed. But her main problem is that she cannot stop smoking because her family finds her impossible to live with when she is not smoking. 'My family find me so irritable that, despite hating smoking themselves, they beg me to go out and buy cigarettes.'

There has been little research into what so many women like Mrs S. are afraid of if they stop smoking. One small study of 16 middle-class housewives attending a stop-smoking programme in Connecticut concluded that one of the main barriers to stopping smoking was indeed a fear of losing control and expressing hostility. One woman on the regime said: 'Getting angry hurts others. When I smoke, I feel a release in my whole body from anger and tension. The cigarette won't hurt anybody but me.' 'Our husbands', said another participant, 'can explode when they come home, but we can't. We are supposed to absorb the frustrations of everyone else in the family and still maintain the image of the superwife and supermother. I don't want to scream and yell at the family and hurt people, so I smoke.'[1] These women vividly express some of the underlying fears that many cannot afford to address, because such a confrontation represents a threat not only to their own sense of marital security, but to that of their husbands and entire family.

Although housewives are still less likely to smoke than women who go out to work, the Connecticut housewives illustrate how hard it is to escape the power of the cigarette. Whilst the housewife's home environment allows her some freedom in how to run her life, there are often no other adults around to respond to her feelings. She must still be the rock of tranquillity for her family and needs her cigarettes to keep her on her best behaviour.

Fear of Getting Fat

> With my smoking now ceasing
> My food was increasing
> And the bills which came in were immense;
> My vital statistics
> Were unrealistic
> Things just didn't seem to make sense.
>
> The problem of dieting
> Was very disquieting,
> I existed for weeks without dinner.
> My physique I exerted
> And snacks I deserted,
> But nothing would make me get thinner.

This 17-year-old girl's musings won her a poetry prize in a magazine for young women.[2] In her own way, she reflects the fears of many women. Not everybody puts on weight when they stop smoking (see page 119), yet being frightened about getting fat prevents many women from stopping smoking. Weight control is also an important motive for *continuing to smoke*. Research has confirmed that twice as many women as men worry about putting on weight when they stop smoking, yet men tend, on average, to gain *more* weight than women when they give up, although this does not seem to worry them unduly.[3] In a survey I conducted of men and women smokers who wrote to ASH for help, by far the commonest reason given for smoking among the women was 'to keep my weight down', whereas this did not emerge as a serious reason among the men. One of the most strikingly consistent features to emerge from my research into why women smoke was that most women who contacted me were either afraid to stop smoking because they thought they would gain weight, or had tried to stop but had gone back to cigarettes because of weight gains.

Susie is 17 and is working for her 'A' levels. To Susie, smoking is a lesser evil than eating. 'I would have a cigarette instead of nibbling and picking at food between meals when I'm not supposed to be hungry anyway . . . to stop smoking would mean not only that I would have to break away from my smoking friends, but that I would go back to picking food from the larder. What is needed is another form of oral satisfaction which has no bad social or health effects.'

Helen is a 21-year-old student who smokes up to 25 cigarettes a day. Although she started at 13 out of bravado (see page 30), she feels she now smokes for quite different reasons. 'One very significant reason is the fear of gaining weight. After a six-week period of giving up, I found my appetite for chocolate and biscuits increased phenomenally. I began smoking again to subdue my appetite. I equate smoking with weight loss.'

Olga is 41 and smokes 20 low-tar cigarettes a day. She responded to the publicity on smoking and health five years ago and stopped. She was delighted she had managed to 'break the habit', but was so afraid of gaining weight that she did not dare eat anything either. 'Imagine the hell. I stuck it for as long as I could— not smoking and hardly eating anything either, but finally succumbed with great remorse and started smoking again, having lost 28 lbs.'

Olga managed an extraordinarily punitive regime for three months, displaying strong—if misdirected—willpower. It had all been channelled into keeping thin.

Many women find they smoke to reduce their weight, and eat compulsively at the same time. Cigarettes help Pauline to get through the day without eating anything, but by the evening she 'can't avoid those horrifying binges where [she] will eat a Mars Bar, a Kit Kat and 14 biscuits with milk.' Pauline recognises that smoking is a serious health risk, but cannot stop because of wanting to control her weight. Yet smoking doesn't control her compulsion to eat and she finds that, despite smoking, she still gains weight. To leave the vicious circle, she must face the prospect of further possible weight gain. Research on 5,000 women attending a weight-reduction course in the US confirms the ineffectiveness of smoking as an appetite-suppressant. In fact, the more overweight the woman, the more heavily is she likely to smoke.[4]

Jane is a 30-year-old architect and smokes up to a pack of cigarettes a day. The fatter she feels, the more she smokes. Sometimes she hardly smokes at all: 'When I feel thin, I can cope with the world, and men in particular. It is only then that I have enough confidence to deal with my male colleagues at work. My cigarettes help me to make up for this ridiculous sense of inadequacy I have. Rationally, I know that I am as intellectually able as my colleagues, but I don't seem able to convince myself of my abilities.'

Jane badly wants to be part of their male world. She competes in the only way she knows how: 'At work I get men to listen to me because I feel thin and attractive. I don't want to be treated as a sex object, yet I can't believe that men will take me seriously. So I force them to pay attention to me through my body. I want to stop smoking but I can't afford to lose the self-respect my thinness gives me. My cigarettes have become my food, my source of strength. My need for food is more threatening to my life than my need for cigarettes.'

Fear of Failure

A 1967 survey of 300 men showed that the successful ex-smoker not only had disapproving attitudes to smoking, but was also likely to be highly confident, a light drinker, and with a firm sense of personal security.[5] A British government survey of both male and female smokers in 1979 showed that, despite equal proportions of men and women *wanting* to stop smoking, women were not as convinced as men of their ability to succeed: two-thirds of the men were inclined to believe in their ability to stop, while only about half the women thought they could succeed.[6]

B. is a former government minister with a special interest in preventive medicine. She smokes 20 cigarettes a day. She managed to stop smoking for a year before taking on her ministerial duties, at a time when she was actively campaigning on smoking and other health issues. Once appointed a minister, she began smoking again intermittently. 'As opportunities and, therefore, pressures in my job grew, I gradually increased my consumption to 20 a day. As a woman in parliament you are in constant competition with men—with men who are confident and assured of their roles as legislators and opinion-leaders. As women parliamentarians, we haven't yet had the time to develop the same confidence. When women speak in the House, they are always well-briefed and have done their homework. They rarely jump up and say anything off the cuff. That is a prerogative that stems from being a confident male.'

As for Jane, smoking is a confidence-barometer for B. The more her competence came under scrutiny, the more she smoked. She felt that any political error would be taken as evidence of her female inferiority: 'I was always beset with the inner worry of never wanting to slip up. If a male colleague slipped up, you could always say it was "bad luck" or an "off day". But if a woman made a mistake, they would say "What else, after all, can you expect from a woman?"'

Since leaving government, B. has returned to her former career as a writer. She still smokes, albeit the lowest-tar cigarettes available. She wants to stop now more than ever, but doesn't yet have the confidence. 'I sit at my desk each morning trying to write. But I don't believe I shall be able to write well, so I smoke instead.' So, like Jane who denied her talents by focusing on her body, B. denies her abilities by smoking instead of writing.

Heather is a 29-year-old clinical psychologist who used to smoke 60 cigarettes a day. She had wanted to stop for years. She began to get increasingly frequent bouts of bronchitis. She was on a student grant, and had to sacrifice holidays and clothes to spend £10 a week on cigarettes. She had no respect for smokers and, as a smoker, was in a minority at work. She made several serious but unsuccessful attempts to stop and even attended a smokers' clinic. She used every trick and diversion she could think of, including rewarding herself, scaring herself, and even disgusting herself by collecting all her cigarette ends in a messy heap in her bedroom. Yet none seemed to have any impact. After she finally succeeded in summer 1978, the reasons for Heather's past failures became clearer: 'I simply didn't feel that I was *ready* to stop at the time or on subsequent occasions ... I knew I was always fighting something in myself during these attempts: that's why I always capitulated to the little voice that said "go on, be nice to yourself, make yourself feel better, you need that fag."' At the time, Heather was depressed. She had her training and qualifying exams to face and felt socially inadequate because she didn't have a boy-friend. Once she had passed her exams and got a good job, life changed radically. 'I suddenly had several reasons to feel good about myself.' She found a new, non-smoking flat-mate and formed a relationship with a man who not only encouraged her to stop, but was prepared to support her efforts to do so. 'I suddenly realised that I really didn't need another cigarette. My friend helped me to tip the scales towards listening to the "third force" in me which said "you are strong, and you don't need to crave that cigarette" . . . This time I knew that *all* of me wanted to stop. I felt convinced that I would succeed . . . Smoking for me was tied up with some very basic feelings of not being able to support myself or "feed" myself adequately. It was my dummy and my badge of defeat. The anti-smoking part of me was the critical voice, the mocking, unhelpful part. I couldn't stop until I felt stronger.'

Unlike Heather, Tanya made her first serious attempt to stop smoking when her confidence was at its lowest ebb. As far as her health was concerned, Tanya had even better reasons than Heather to stop: her doctor had told her after her second child was born that if she carried on smoking, she would be dead in ten years. Tanya had a chronic cough with a persistent pain in the chest. She went to a local smokers' clinic, but managed to stay off cigarettes for only two-and-a-half weeks. The key factors preventing success in her case were a lack of confidence in her ability to maintain resolve and 13 years of unhappy marriage. 'Even when I stopped, I never dared think I'd be able to stay off permanently. I kept thinking in terms of weeks, and then going back to cigarettes.' Tanya felt her husband's attitude also undermined her self-confidence. 'I didn't feel as if I was getting any encouragement from him. He thought going to the clinic was stupid. He didn't see why I couldn't manage on my own. He thought I should be able to click my fingers and stop—just like him. He always seems to me to be the kind of person who is always able to do what he wants to do. He gave up smoking for three months because he wanted to, and he started again because he wanted to.'

In the first two weeks after stopping, Tanya gained some weight, which reduced her confidence even further—her husband had told her how 'horrible and fat' she had become after having her second baby. She then discovered that he had secretly been going out with another woman, who had become pregnant. She threw him out of the house and took up cigarettes again.

6. A Society that Keeps Women Smoking

Is it possible, from the pieces of evidence we have gathered so far, to offer a general explanation of why women smoke? According to the experts, smoking in women is an inevitable result of their growing emancipation. The cigarette is, in their view, 'a symbol of emancipation' and 'a defiant gesture of independence'.[1,2] The American National Institute of Drug Abuse (NIDA) believes that, as we move towards equality in education and work, women's smoking patterns reflect that equality. 'Smoking', says NIDA, 'may be perceived in some way as an indicator of increased power and independence.'[3] Some researchers go further and suggest that women smoke to 'increase their identification with the masculine mode of relating to the world.'[4] The assumption implicit in these conclusions is that the rise of smoking among women over the last 15 years is a consequence of the parallel rise of the feminist movement of the 1960s.

There is little evidence to support this. First, we have already seen (page 14) that it is nonsense to suggest that women are in some way less aware of smoking hazards than men. And it is clear that more women started smoking, and smoking more, long before the women's movement began to have any impact. But, more importantly, there is no evidence that women who smoke are any more likely to be feminists than are non-smokers. The American Cancer Society conducted a survey in 1977 which showed that women who were non-smokers were just as likely as women who smoked to identify with the women's movement.[5]

The Two Sides of the Woman-Smoker Equation

It would, of course, be naïve to assume that changing attitudes towards women have had no influence on women's smoking habits, for they have certainly contributed to removing the old taboos against female smokers. But it is quite wrong to go on— without any evidence whatsoever—to condemn the growth of the women's movement for the rise in women's smoking, and to assume that women want to become like men and, therefore, smoke like men.

There are two processes shaping women's smoking patterns today. First, there are the factors which have led girls to catch up and even to overtake boys in the frequency with which they are starting to smoke. The influences at work here owe much to the new climate of liberation. But we must not confuse them with the factors influencing the difficulties women have in giving up smoking. The key to understanding this second part of the problem stems not so much from our new equalities, but from continuing *inequalities*.

A Glimmer of Liberation

As we have already seen, smoking to the teenager becomes a symbol of liberation from childhood and parental controls. For boys, smoking has always symbolised entry into the tough male world which promises power and sexual adventure. Boys who smoke tend to be more rebellious, impulsive and anti-authority than their non-smoking classmates. For boys, cigarette smoking forms part of the image expected of them. It is an image that says: 'I'm cool and daring; I've had sexual experience.' This does not, of course, fit the stereotypical image of girls. According to convention, girls are supposed to be quiet, demure and co-operative. Industriousness, obedience and, above all, virginity are qualities highly prized in girls; smoking patterns in girls bore out this stereotype—until recently. Fewer girls than boys smoked, and girls started smoking much later than boys. In the late 1960s, research showed that girls took a highly moralistic attitude to smoking: they strongly disapproved of other girls (but not boys) smoking. Ten years later, this was no longer the case.[6] Girls now smoke as much and, in some cases, more than boys (see pages 11–12). Smoking, for some girls, has become a defiant rejection of society's stereotypical female image. Girls are now showing, in greater numbers, that they can be as rebellious, daring and anti-establishment as boys.[7]

But this new emancipation is usually short-lived. At a relatively early age, girls who smoke begin to show the tell-tale signs that mark their future difficulties as smokers.

For instance, Annie, who started smoking when she was 11 (see page 32). Her reasons for smoking were—even at that age—related to the many insecurities women experience in adulthood.

'I began smoking because it helped a very overweight and insecure child with no real friends to feel daring and important. At school I could never maintain best-friend status with any one person, but when I went off to the park with my cigarettes, people came with me.' Annie is still battling with her weight problem—and her cigarettes.

A decade of change in society's attitudes to men and women has hardly been sufficient to eradicate the different expectations society has of boys and girls and they have of themselves. The American Cancer Society study showed that girls are more worried than boys about the hazards of smoking. Young boys who smoke still see smoking as an asset, while girls do not. And there are signs that the girls half-regret starting, so they try harder than the boys to cut down.[8] And tradition dies hard. Recent research in Britain shows that boys who smoke tend to view themselves as 'tough', 'clever' and 'good-looking' far more frequently than do their more diffident, female counterparts.[9]

Teaching Women to Be Addicted

How does the carefree, liberated teenage girl, who can take or leave cigarettes, develop into a woman who craves cigarettes? Like many girls, Tanya used to smoke out of bravado. Now, one husband and two children later, she has a different story to tell: 'I used to smoke because I wanted to; now I need to.' What are these needs that Tanya and so many other women talk about?

Take Mrs D. who smoked occasionally as a young woman, but never felt deprived or particularly in need of cigarettes when she was at work where smoking wasn't allowed. 'My true addiction began', she says, 'when my husband broke out in a rash [sic] of schizophrenia. No help was available to us then [20 years ago] and the tensions became unbearable.' From then on, Mrs D.'s life was punctuated by her husband's deterioration and periodic stays in hospital. She managed to stop smoking quite easily following a serious stroke which involved staying in hospital for some time. 'I did not think of smoking again until my husband's aggro one day sent me rushing to buy cigarettes.' Mrs D. has smoked 20 a day ever since. Although Mrs D. is convinced she is addicted, she sees her addiction in its social context: 'I think I smoke from boredom and despair, there being no foreseeable end to my marriage predicament.' Although Mrs D.'s difficulties are in some ways extreme, her account clearly illustrates the social origins of her need to smoke. While cigarettes do have demonstrable chemical effects, the strength of a smoker's 'addiction' is very much a reflection of how addicted they *perceive* themselves to be. These preconceptions will be profoundly influenced by what they have learned, directly or indirectly, from society's experts. Thus, if society, taking a lead from the medical profession, views cigarette smoking as a form of addiction, this is precisely what the smoker is likely to believe. Smoking is usually regarded as a medical problem, and the notion of addiction has become locked within the physical confines of disease—a 'sickness' for which doctors must find a 'cure'. Many a well-meaning doctor or health educator has inadvertently helped to create the addiction they are so anxious to cure. The more convinced a smoker is about being an addict, the less likely they are to be able to stop smoking. The addict uses addiction as a justification, not for stopping, but for *continuing* to smoke.

But why are women so much more convinced about their addiction to cigarettes than are men? Why are the ASH mailbag and smokers' clinics filled with requests from women who are sure of their hopeless dependence? Linda is 25 and has smoked for seven years. She did stop for three months, but went back to it because she gained weight. As far as Linda is concerned, the whole problem is beyond her control. She feels unable to do anything about her smoking. 'I can see no way of giving up unless I am given a severe fright or made to feel thoroughly ashamed. This places the effort squarely in somebody else's court when I know I should be able to do it on my own.' Linda's plea captures the essence of what addiction is about for women. It is about giving in to forces beyond your control, letting cigarettes rule your life for you. And, more importantly, it is about feeling unable to cope with problems on your own. It is about helplessness and dependence. The woman who depends on her tranquillisers for survival may also depend on her cigarettes. Is it coincidental, for example, that twice as many women as men take tranquillisers and that those who work part-time (mainly women) take more tranquillisers than any other occupational group?[10] Is it also chance that women who smoke also drink more alcohol?[11] And take more of every category of mood-changing drug than non-smokers?[12]

Our kind of society makes it much easier for a woman to fall into the role of the helpless dependent addict than for a man. Women's addiction-training starts early in life. The American Cancer Society's teenage study showed that girls are more

43

convinced than boys that smoking is an addiction.[13] Behind this attitude lie the roots of the difficulty women experience in stopping smoking. Research into general attitudes to health indicates that as early as six years old, boys see themselves as strong and less susceptible to illness than are girls. Girls, by contrast, feel more vulnerable, and are more likely to seek help.[14,15] Every boy learns quickly that he must 'take his pain like a man'— crying is for sissies and girls. By the time children leave school, girls are already well-primed for addiction and dependence. Younger men characteristically take the view that they are not addicted and can stop any time. By contrast, women are quicker to admit to being 'hopelessly addicted'.

Keeping Feelings under Control

Once a confirmed 'addict', a woman incorporates her smoking into her constant battle for control over her emotions and so-called 'irrational' feelings (see chapter 5). Feeling in control of their lives is, of course, just as important to men as it is to women. But the ways open to women to exert this control are more limited than for men. A man has greater scope for control through his job and the associated status and responsibility he derives as the 'breadwinner'. He may also exert it at home, over how his pay packet is spent or how often he and his wife have sex. Even though increasing numbers of women—especially married women—also have jobs, persistent inequalities both at work and at home mean that the spheres of potential control open to a woman lie largely within the family and the personal. *It is more important for a woman to be seen to be keeping her emotions in check than for a man*, because she has, in political terms, so little influence over other aspects of her life. If she fails to do so, she has little else to fall back on, whereas her occasionally unruly or drunken husband still has his influence outside the home, both at work and at play. The more fulfilling his outside activities, the more he can afford to ignore any failures of control in his personal life. Smoking, like dieting, is therefore one of the few ways open to the majority of women to attempt to prove that they are in control of their personal lives. Which is why it is also crucial for women to use smoking to try to control their body weight.

Undermining our Confidence

To deal with her smoking, a woman must believe in her ability to control her urge to smoke. The successful ex-smoker has a highly developed sense of independence and a strong drive to achieve specific goals.[16] Research shows that men commonly over-estimate their ability to achieve any set task, an attitude which acts to *maximise* their performance in that particular task. Thus, if we assume that the self-confidence required to stop smoking successfully stems from a person's self-esteem, it is easy to see why men are more successful at it than women. For the same research shows that women hold a low opinion of themselves and perceive themselves to be less competent than men under most circum-stances.[17] While there is little difference in this respect between young girls and boys, the 'competence gap' grows as they approach adulthood.[18] Thus, the lack of confidence in their ability to stop smoking successfully, which many women express, is but one manifestation of society's failure to encourage women to value themselves highly.

The Need to be Thin

Nearly all women—smokers and non-smokers alike—want to be thin. Being thin has a meaning for women that it does not have for men. Women are under constant pressure to squeeze themselves into clothes that are too small, because we live in a society that values women largely for what we look like—not what we do. Current western fashions dictate that to be beautiful you have to be thin; thus thinness is one of the few sources of self-esteem society allows women.[19] Although smoking is not a passport to weight loss, and giving up does not necessarily result in weight gain, women smokers often equate smoking with being thin and in control. Giving up, therefore, represents a threat to a woman's badly needed self-esteem. She sees her smoking as a means of maintaining her self-confidence in a world where she feels she has to be thin to be successful in her relationships with men. It is easy to see why she might believe that being thin is more important than stopping smoking. It is not because she doesn't recognise that smoking is far more damaging to health than the possibility of putting on weight, but that she has been forced to view controlling her weight *as a more immediate priority*. The thought of being fat, undesired and unsuccessful seems far more difficult to face than the prospect of becoming ill from smoking at some undefined future date.

7. A Question of Conflict

> I'm not a women's libber, but I do feel that women
> have to give more of themselves in this life than
> men. The majority of women work at a full-time
> job, and then accomplish miracles in the house—
> cleaning, shopping, cooking and laundry etc. in the
> few short hours left in the day. Their husbands
> often help, but the ultimate responsibility for
> decisions made in connection with organising a
> home rests with the woman of the house. I don't
> honestly think a woman has time to concentrate on
> trying to give up smoking.

This is how Alison understands the difficulty she and other women smokers experience. Alison is 48 and works as a full-time secretary to the director of a small engineering firm. 'I am also a "girl Friday" at the office, and have to worry about everything in the running of a smooth operation from the most detailed of confidential correspondence to ensuring there is enough toilet paper.'

Smoking became a serious problem for Alison four years before her husband died. At 25 cigarettes a day, she was 'beginning to feel the stress and strain of the rat-race, especially holding down a full-time job and running a home.' She reached a stage where she 'couldn't seem to relax even when there was an opportunity'. Since her husband's death, it has become increasingly difficult to make ends meet. 'There is always the nagging fear at the back of my mind of being out of work, and wondering how I would manage. I get mentally tired at work and don't feel like tackling any domestic work when I go home.'

Alison used to enjoy running her home when her husband was alive, but postpones housework for as long as possible now so that she can keep up with the demands of work outside the home. She desperately wants to stop smoking. 'I hate myself for doing it, and feel constantly guilty about not being able to stop.' The difficulty for Alison is not so much the stopping itself, but staying off cigarettes. 'I always revert back to cigarettes because the alternative is to get fired from my job or to crash my car.' Known as Auntie Alison by her workmates, she feels she has to live up to her gentle calm image. Her cigarettes are the only outward sign of the inner harassment she often feels.

Alison's need to smoke is a gauge of the conflict of loyalties in her life. If she devotes time and effort to stopping and staying off cigarettes, she must ignore other demands. Alison's predicament is familiar to most women smokers. She is torn by conflicting social pressures that maintain her need to smoke. And they are not the same as the pressures on most men.

Philippa is 37, and runs a holiday home for underprivileged children. She smokes 20 cigarettes a day. She has a non-smoking husband and three children who regularly put pressure on her to stop smoking. Family pressures seemed to work—for a while at least—in 1977. But a disaster at home brought her rushing back to cigarettes. 'We were flooded out at home for three weeks, and I couldn't cope, fighting the craving for cigarettes *and* running the home.' Philippa has clear ideas about why women need cigarettes. 'The biggest factor in women's lives is stress. Smoking is highest in poor areas. So is stress. More women are taking on the responsibilities that men traditionally carried alone. And more women are smoking: stress again. Many women in creative careers smoke. Creating is stressful if you've got a family to think about too.'

Philippa's answer is certainly an oversimplification. But there is good reason to believe that smoking patterns do reflect— at least in part—the amount of stress in people's lives. The more stressed a person feels, the more difficult it seems to be for them to stop smoking. For a woman, marriage and family responsibilities usually re-shape any hopes she may have for herself. Society still expects her to devote herself primarily to her children and her husband, thus maximising the conflict between pursuing a career and caring for her family. The cigarettes many women can't seem to stop lighting are one of the outward signs of their attempts to cope with that stress as best they can.

The Happy Housewife?

The more out of line you are with the demands of society, the greater your sense of conflict and the more likely you are to feel the need to smoke.

Sarah is 26, and spends most of her time at home looking after her baby. She smokes between 20 and 30 cigarettes a day. She badly wants to stop and has made 'countless' attempts to do so. She describes herself as 'completely dependent' on tobacco. 'The guy I live with—the one with the income—is careless about money, and we always run short about the middle of the month. One month there was only just enough left for food—I just had to stop smoking. I was full of helpless rage and bitterness at being brought so low by his improvidence. In the end I adapted and managed by scrounging six cigarettes a day.'

But Sarah soon returned to her former 20 a day. She sees her smoking as 'stupid and needless', yet she feels that women in her position need to smoke. 'A cigarette is the only pleasure you can indulge in without the kids pestering you for their share— especially if you've had no break from them for hours or days and couldn't afford to go out even if you did have a babysitter. You're tired, they're whiny, bored and awful. Ten fags may be the only pleasure you can (just) afford. They are your substitute for leisure, pleasure and ordinary adult activities.'

Women from the Birmingham Women and Health Group saw smoking in a similar light. They smoked most when minding their children. Smoking, they felt, 'enables a woman to separate herself off from her children. The children have to wait until their mother finishes her cigarette. It makes her feel different and 'grown up', because smoking is an adult activity. It is a treat to relieve the monotony of being at home with small children all day.'

Sarah and the women from Birmingham describe the isolation and lack of stimulation many mothers feel while looking after young and demanding children. Many women willingly give up their jobs to have children, but they are not accustomed to the lack of support from other adults and the unchanging, yet demanding routine of the world of babies. Most rapidly become aware of the conflict between their desire to be good mothers and the stress they feel, which can express itself through smoking or other means such as tranquillisers or alcohol. It comes as no surprise, therefore, that those housewives who do smoke find it harder to stop than do other women.[1]

Career and Children: An Incompatible Marriage?

Myra is 46. She has four children, and a non-smoking husband. She works for her local Family Planning Association as a 'general dog's-body', and is taking a full-time course in social work. Myra is convinced of the risks to her health. Her husband and children have all put pressure on her to stop. Yet she continues to smoke 40 cigarettes a day. Why? She is convinced that she is addicted to tobacco and is unable to muster the willpower to stop. Yet she sees her addiction not in chemical, but in social terms, and has noticed that she is not alone with her cigarette problem.

'My friends and colleagues at work are mainly women under the double pressure of work and home commitments. They are all smokers. They devote a lot of time to half-hearted methods of cutting down. On the other hand, I have known several men who seem to have been able to give up with the greatest of ease.'

Myra has to fight a battle to balance priorities between her own work and her children's and her husband's needs. 'I desperately don't want to bring up latch-key children. I have to try to combine being a good mother with keeping up with the work expected of me at college. My husband doesn't like me working and would much prefer me to be the little woman at home. He is often disgruntled and feels hard-done-by if meals aren't ready on time and the house is untidy. Although he is happy to benefit from the extra pay packet I bring home, he still wants to play the conventional male role where he dominates and I take charge of domestic chores.' Myra's thoughts reflect the experience of every mother who faces the problem of finding childcare during her working day. Will they suffer from so-called 'maternal deprivation'? Should she be leaving them at all? Deadlines at work seldom make allowances for motherhood, and the anxiety generated by these pressures can often be measured by the amount a women smokes. It is no accident that smoking rates among women who are most uneasy with this two-role conflict are as high, and sometimes higher than among men.

Ms Independent

What of the so-called independent career woman—so beloved of the advertising men? For many such women, smoking becomes an indispensable means of hiding the underlying stress imposed by a society that disapproves of the choices they have made. Barbara fits the bill as 'Ms Independent'. At 28, she is ambitious and competent in her work as an architect. There is every chance that she will be promoted alongside the best of her male colleagues. Yet beneath the tough exterior, she feels insecure and has a constant nagging sense of being unfulfilled. She is not married and sees her smoking as a sign of failure—a feeling aggravated by her being the only woman working with four male architects who neither smoke nor approve of her smoking.

'I look around in my office and see that my male colleagues are married with children. They seem to experience a kind of contentment I have never known, which makes me feel even more abnormal. Most of my female friends have left their jobs to have children. I think I find it hard to come to terms with the idea that if I pursue my career with the kind of single-mindedness that this male-orientated profession demands, I may never have time for children. Nobody has ever said that I've got the wrong priorities; they just think it. It makes me feel even more ill-at-ease with the choices facing me. I either settle down and have children, which means sacrificing my career, or I follow my ambitions much like my male colleagues. The difference between them and me is that they are doing what is considered to be the norm in our society, and I am going against the grain. I suppose there must be something in me which chooses to oppose accepted female norms. I enjoy my work, but I feel restless at the same time because I feel I ought to be settling down. I feel tense at work, so I smoke. I feel lonely at home, so I smoke. In fact, I think I smoke wherever I feel abnormal because I am not somebody's wife or mother.'

8. Hospitals—A Microcosm of Male Dominance

The hospital provides us with a clear illustration of how social forces shape the smoking habits of those who work within an institution. As yet, there has been no research into the smoking habits of non-professional hospital workers, but the smoking patterns found among doctors and nurses clearly reflect the consequences of working within a society where workers are divided not only by race and class, but also by sex. It is true that both doctors and nurses have a double incentive to stop smoking. Not only do they repeatedly see the effects of cigarette-induced disease, but they are expected to set an example to the community. Doctors, it seems, have responded to this pressure, so that only one in five of them still smokes, compared with just under one in every two men in the rest of the population.[1] But nearly half of all hospital nurses smoke, a much higher proportion than the average for women in the population as a whole.[2] Not only are nurses' smoking rates twice as high as those of their medical colleagues, they also have only half the doctors' success rates for stopping smoking.[3] This pattern is not peculiar to the British health system. American and Australian research has yielded the same results.[4,5] Indeed, in the USA there are signs that smoking among nurses has been growing, while other health professionals have been giving up.[6]

Not only do relatively few nurses stop smoking successfully; more nurses are taking it up. A recent survey of nursing students in training in Edinburgh showed that, as a young female nurse progresses through her training, she is *more* rather than less likely to start smoking. In the first year, 18 per cent of the students smoked; but this proportion shot up to 60 per cent by the third year of training.[7] Medical students also show some increases in the proportion who smoke as they advance through their training, but this increase is far less dramatic and is now showing signs of disappearing.[8,9]

Why Do So Many Nurses Smoke?

If doctors and medical students can stay off cigarettes, why can't nurses? Anti-smoking campaigners have been quick to suggest that nurses are either less aware of the health hazards of smoking or less likely to accept them. But recent surveys in the UK and the USA show that although doctors were better-informed about the more specific effects of smoking, nine in every ten doctors *and* nurses recognised that smoking caused ill-health.[10,11] And the differences cannot be explained on the basis of age differences between doctors and nurses, because nurses have higher smoking rates *in every age group* than do any other health professionals.

How then can we explain these differences? Class differences between doctors and nurses contribute, because nurses are much more likely than doctors to come from working-class backgrounds —despite the fact that they are classified as 'professionals' alongside doctors in British government statistics. Yet class alone cannot explain why nurses have even higher smoking rates than their working-class counterparts in other jobs. Perhaps nurses

51

smoke because of the stress of the job itself. Certainly, working in a hospital is emotionally demanding. Although research is limited, smoking does seem to be a good barometer of high-stress specialities. In psychiatry, for example, where the emotional demands on staff are high, both doctors and nurses have the highest smoking rates of all; rates are also high in paediatrics where staff may work in special premature baby units with the constant stress of frequent deaths.[12] In a survey of nurses' smoking habits in the Leeds area, smoking rates proved to be highest among those working in cancer wards where staff know that much of the treatment is only palliative, and that many of their patients will not recover.[13]

But these specific stresses still do not explain why the discrepancy between nurses' and doctors' smoking habits is so great. Are stresses on nurses different or greater than those on doctors? According to American research, nursing is more stressful—as measured by the incidence of mental illness—than most other occupations.[14] The nurse normally takes on the responsibility for caring for the sick and dying at a much earlier stage than her medical counterpart. And, unlike the doctor, when on duty she is trapped on the ward with little freedom of action or control over her own activities. The resulting stresses are quite different from those experienced by doctors. On duty, the nurse is faced with a series of crises punctuated by long periods of boredom—especially at night. Smoking becomes one of the few ways a nurse can relieve her boredom or frustration without leaving the ward. Some groups of nurses appear to be relatively immune to the lure of the cigarette, particularly those who work in the community, only a quarter of whom smoke.[15] Unlike the ward nurse, the community nurse has autonomy, responsibility and, above all, freedom to work with her patients as she sees fit. The hospital nurse, however, works under the double hierarchy of medical and nursing authority and, as the daily frustrations pile up, she resorts, like other women, to cigarettes.

Women Doctors—The Missing Link?

We might expect women doctors' smoking habits to reflect those of their male colleagues. Yet, while women doctors have been more successful than other women in resisting smoking or in giving it up, they have not, on the whole, been as successful as their male colleagues. Not only do women doctors find it harder to stop smoking than do men, but there is evidence that the proportion of American women doctors who smoke may have *overtaken* the male total in recent years.[16] And recent surveys in New Zealand suggest that more women doctors are smoking while their male colleagues are giving up.[17]

From the limited research available, it seems clear there are stresses that are common to both nurses and women doctors which make their smoking problem more difficult to surmount than that of their male colleagues. Class differences and the specific stresses of a nurse's job may, in part, explain her need to smoke, but we must also remember that the medical profession is as quintessentially male as the nursing profession is female. About three-quarters of British doctors are men, and nine in every ten nurses are women. Even a casual glance at who is most likely to smoke in the health service reveals that the lower-status your job, the higher your smoking rates, *and* that *most of the lowest-status jobs are occupied by women*. The lower you go in the nursing hierarchy, the less likely you are to find men and the more likely you are to find high smoking rates. Although estimates vary, one 1979 survey showed that as many as 54 per cent of nursing auxiliaries—right at the bottom of the nursing hierarchy—smoke, compared with only 31 per cent of fully-trained nurses.[18]

But the most important factor is that nursing is women's work, and, like women in other jobs, nurses are underpaid and undervalued. Many qualified nurses with several years' experience are forced to live under the constraints of hospital accommodation because they cannot afford to live anywhere else. Nursing bears the female label of nurturing, caring and, above all, serving others, while being regarded as menial. Although a nurse's work is as essential to the well-being of the patient as a doctor's, nurses are regarded as doctors' hand-maidens or assistants. The mounting anger that many nurses feel, at their subordination within a health service dependent on women but operated by men, can be gauged by the thickness of the smoke emerging from nurses' offices.

Beryl is a 25-year old mature student nurse. She stopped smoking before she started training, but used to smoke 20 a day when she was a nursing auxiliary. Beryl is committed to becoming a nurse, but resents the power structure within the hospital and paints an uncompromising picture of life on the ward: 'You are always the underdog, at the bottom of the pecking order. We have little control over our work. It is always determined by the nurse above us and the nurse above her. I resent being looked upon as a glorified waitress instead of the professional I'm training to become . . . you are conscious of being just a nurse—you simply don't exist. In nursing you quickly realise that medicine is a separate camp—and a more powerful camp than ours. We usually carry out what the doctor says we should do. Which I accept as correct. But I also think that we do a helluva lot that we don't get credit for. Patients are thankful, but professionals are not. It creates the impression that nurses are dispensable and doctors are not.'

The Unequal Woman Doctor

There are some encouraging signs that the number of women doctors is increasing—nearly half of British medical students now entering training are female—but the tell-tale features of continuing inequality remain and are reflected in women doctors' smoking patterns. The higher a man rises in the medical hierarchy, the less likely he is to smoke, but the opposite is true of women. A survey of the smoking habits of women doctors who had graduated from Johns Hopkins University in the USA showed that nearly 60 per cent of those who had become professors smoked, compared with 37 per cent of more junior female colleagues.[19] How can we explain these alarmingly high smoking rates? Success for the women professors clearly meant choosing between a career and marriage. Nearly half the professors were unmarried, while all the women doctors who had ceased to practice were married. The women not in practice had an average of four children, compared with less than two among the professors. The survey also found that the professors had little time to feel depressed, but had higher anxiety levels than all other groups.[20]

In addition to a conflict of loyalties, women doctors also face an aggressively competitive male hierarchy. In the USA, for example, male doctors still out-number females by nine to one, and there is little room for gentle 'feminine' attributes in the businesslike world of American medicine. The system requires doctors to sell themselves aggressively and, above all, to be supremely confident. Although there are more women doctors in Britain, a quick glance at the sex distribution of doctors in the various specialities shows that a large proportion of women work in the least 'glamorous' specialities such as psychiatry, geriatrics

54

and pathology, while the cardiologists and surgeons are almost all men. Women doctors, like nurses, do not yet have the confidence or the power to secure more humane working hours, training schemes and nursery provision at work. Their smoking can, therefore, be seen as one way of expressing their impotence and dissatisfaction at working in an institution which does not recognise some of their most basic needs.

Lorraine is a 32-year old senior registrar in radiotherapy (radiation treatment for cancer) at a London teaching hospital. Her growing dependence on cigarettes reflects the pressures on her as both a woman *and* a doctor. She smoked occasionally as a teenager 'because it was naughty', and as a medical student because everyone else did. It was not until she started working as a qualified doctor at 24 that smoking became a serious problem. In her first year as a junior doctor, her duty rota left her with little more freedom that that of a nurse. She was on duty all night every other night, which meant being in the hospital 120 hours a week: 'I don't think I had a decent night's sleep all year. When you were up at 4 a.m. and had to keep awake, you smoked, drank and ate sausage rolls. I became addicted to cigarettes and to food. In that constant awful busy life of the houseman [junior doctor], smoking was no longer naughty, it was a treat, a way of punctuating the never-ending demands of the day.' She now hates to be seen smoking and hardly ever smokes at work: 'I find it very embarrassing. It is a hideous thing to do. I am anxious not to be seen smoking at work. I want to project a better image of myself. I don't want them to see how stressed I am. My desire not to be seen smoking is like not wanting to be seen demolishing a plate of peanuts at a party when I'm on a diet—it's a sign of being out of control.'

Lorraine believes that the stresses on women doctors are 'certainly greater' than those on men. She describes the pressure of continually having to prove her ability in a world where women are always wrong until proven right. And there is also the pressure of not feeling free to express her feelings for fear of being labelled hysterical. 'I constantly felt at a disadvantage because I was female. It has improved a bit in recent years, but you *had* to be better than the men to get jobs at London teaching hospitals. In a place like a hospital, where you're always being measured up against men, there is a definite feeling of having to be more excellent, which is tough on you because it means not having children or possibly postponing having them until later. I'd always assumed that, when I was older, I'd have children and go on working full-time. I am now not so sure that it would be fair to my children. I'm beginning to feel I have cheated people at job interviews, because you have to say that if you ever have children you would continue doing a full day's work to get the job. I feel guilty for having competed with men for the best jobs in radiotherapy under false pretences, because I've always said until now that it was as worthwhile to train me as it was a man. Another woman at work with two children has brought it home to me very powerfully—how torn you can become between children and work. I realise that if I were she, I would start to resent the job because it kept me away from the children, and vice versa . . .

'Most of the women doctors I know manage to keep a calm exterior. They have to. They keep all their volatile feelings locked within their private lives. Women doctors are not allowed to have what the men call "temper tantrums"—even when you can see that they are stretched to cracking point. They are always accused of being more emotional than the men. All a woman has to do is say the mildest thing to be classed as bitchy or pre-menstrual. But the men can blow up when they like, kick the secretary in the teeth and be rude to the patients. That's OK. They somehow have a whole outlet that is forbidden for us.'

Being a woman in an overwhelmingly male profession exacerbates the stress that already exists in most women's lives. Lorraine's inability to part with her cigarettes is symptomatic of the same inequalities that confront the nurse who can't stop smoking.

9. The Ladykillers—US Style

Of the many personal and social factors promoting cigarette dependence, cigarette advertising is, perhaps, the most obvious. Nobody likes to admit they are influenced by advertising. But if you do smoke, stop for a moment and think back to what decided you to buy your first pack of cigarettes. How did you view the cigarettes you first bought? Were they an extension of your personality, and your sexuality? Did you really buy those first cigarettes out of a deep-seated need to smoke? Or did you perhaps choose long, sophisticated cigarettes because they looked 'right' when you offered them to friends? How can some cigarettes be regarded as synonymous with charm and sophistication and others with rugged masculinity when all contain the same lethal product?

In tracing the history of cigarette advertising, there can be no doubt that it has and still does play a central role in creating and shaping the preferences of each generation of women (and men) smokers. Until the mid-1920s, the tobacco companies aimed their advertising campaigns only at men. Only a 'debauched' woman or an eccentric actress would dare to smoke in those early post-Victorian days. But the 1920s brought women new freedoms, and American tobacco companies quickly recognised the potential of the female market. American Tobacco was the first company to cash in on it. By using the slogan, 'Reach for a Lucky instead of a sweet,' it was able to sell cigarettes to women as an alleged means of losing weight. In a series of massive advertising campaigns, the company appealed directly to women, using testimonials from well-known women such as Amelia Earhart, the famous flyer, and actress Jean Harlow. Within two years of the 1925 launch, women had helped make 'Lucky Strike' America's best-selling brand.

The tobacco advertisers' tactics haven't changed much, except that they are investing more money than ever before in selling their product. In 1977, for every dollar spent on the anti-smoking campaign, the tobacco companies spent $900 on cigarette advertising.[1] Because US cigarette advertising is almost as uncontrollable today as it was fifty years ago, it provides us with the clearest insight into the tactics tobacco companies use. American advertisers are typically blunt about the steadily-growing purchasing power of the so-called 'new woman'. 'She is', according to the trade papers, 'the hottest marketing target in the US today.'[2]

Women's Magazines: Profit before Health

What better direct route to the 'new woman's' heart than through the channel of the successful women's magazines? More than eight in every ten women read women's magazines and, since cigarette advertisements were banned on US TV in 1971, the magazines

57

have never had it so good. Between 1970 and 1974, annual expenditure on cigarette advertisements in magazines rose from $50 million to a staggering $115 million,[3] and only *Good Housekeeping* refuses cigarette adverts, on the grounds that they are incompatible with editorial policy on health. Indeed, *Good Housekeeping*, unlike its competitors, not only carries frequent articles on smoking and health issues, but recently co-sponsored, with the American Cancer Society, the first national conference on women and cancer. *McCalls*, on the other hand, receives hefty income from cigarette advertising. Over four million women— many of them teenagers—read *Redbook*, which reports a five-fold increase in revenue from cigarette adverts since the TV ban. *Redbook*'s advertising director was quite happy to accept cigarette adverts 'as long as they were not misleading'. In his view, neither advertisers nor audience should be censored.

The growing interest in health promotion in the US has led to the development of several successful women's magazines devoted almost exclusively to health. *Self* magazine describes its objectives as 'helping contemporary women solve the problems created by their new way of life'. Its advertising director explained that it did not refuse cigarette advertisements, though they wouldn't be placed *next* to articles on health or fitness. *Mademoiselle*—for 'millions of women who believe in good health, good looks and good living'—also appears to see no conflict between these aims and the large number of cigarette adverts it regularly carries.

A Study in Hypocrisy

Cigarette advertisements have proliferated, particularly in the magazines directed at the 'emancipated woman'. Every month, more than six million women read *Cosmopolitan* and *Ms*, the two most important contenders for the 'liberated' market. '*Cosmo*', with its aggressively 'feminine' line, reaches readers as young as 14, and as many as one in five of its full-page adverts are for cigarettes. *Ms*, which claims to 'serve women as people, not roles', has firm ideas about advertising. Sexist advertisements, they say, are out, as are 'product categories which may be harmful'. *Ms* has shown its integrity by refusing to accept adverts for vaginal deodorants for these two reasons, and Nina Finkelstein, one of the *Ms* editors, told me of their concern about the possible harm these deodorants could do. America's watchdog, the Food and Drug Administration, certainly warned that vaginal deodorants can cause harmful side-effects such as itching and inflammation—in one in every two million cases.[4] Cigarettes, on the other hand, simply kill one in every four smokers. Yet *Ms* is reluctant to extend its principles of advertising practice to cigarettes. They bring in too much revenue—up to three in every ten full-page ads in *Ms* are for cigarettes.

Ms is critical of magazines that subordinate their editorial content to advertisers' demands. Yet in the eight years since it was launched, it has never carried an article on smoking and health. Nina Finkelstein says an article was planned at one stage, 'but it didn't work out'. The magazine did, however, refuse to accept advertisements for 'Virginia Slims' cigarettes which carried the slogan, 'You've come a long way, baby!' on the grounds that 'baby' was a sexist form of address. Ms Finkelstein explained that had Philip Morris (the manufacturer) been prepared to remove 'baby' from its advertisements, then *Ms* would have happily accepted them—and the $80,000 they would have brought in.

Lured into the 'Low-Tar' Trap

Today's woman smoker has been raised on lower-tar cigarettes. Advertisements for these 'lights', as they are called, are directed at both men and women, but they have special appeal for women. Besides distracting attention from the central health issues and implying that it is safe to smoke lower-tar cigarettes, they also create the subconscious impression that *being* 'light' or 'lean' is part and parcel of smoking long, lean 'lights'. In 1977, American tobacco companies devoted half their advertising budget—nearly $450 million—to advertising lower-tar cigarettes[5] and it has become normal practice to spend anything up to $40 million launching brands such as *Real* and *Now*, which are heavily advertised in women's magazines.[6]

A closer look at the low-tar market shows that 'low tar' is not quite as low as it would seem. The cigarette brands that yield the lowest tar levels (less than 5mg/cigarette) are not the most popular. Many of the brands heavily advertised in women's magazines yield three times more tar than the lowest-tar brand available. Although the shift to lower-tar cigarettes will probably mean that the death toll from smoking in women will never reach the proportions recorded for men, it has also swept fears about their harmful effects well under the carpet. The industry expects what the tobacco trade press calls a 'healthy future', but many women may be misled into believing that smoking low-tar cigarettes is a valid alternative to giving up.

The Evolution of the Female Cigarette

Cigarette advertisements increasingly directed at women, have escaped the notice of feminists campaigning to remove sexist stereotyping in advertising. Ironically, this is because cigarette advertisements rarely portray women in overtly dumb-blonde or passive roles. The National Advertising Review Board (NARB), part of whose job it is to make recommendations on 'matters of taste and social responsibility' in connection with US advertising, specified 14 negative and undesirable (or sexist) ways in which current advertisements portray women. Of these, I could find only three which cigarette adverts breached. Furthermore, the ads actually fulfilled six of the nine proposals from the NARB on how women could be portrayed constructively.[7]

Although there are still many cigarette ads that portray women as sex objects, the cigarette advertisers have done what many other advertisers—and nearly all health educators—have not yet managed to do: they take women seriously. The women in the most successful advertisements are depicted as independent people with their own lives and interests. Today's woman, say the adverts, knows how to get her own cigarette.

The Three-Line Attack
Strategy No. 1: Macho

Apart from the spirited campaigns directed at women in the 1920s and 1930s, the post-war image of the cigarette was predominantly male—until recently. Why did increasing numbers of women begin to smoke a product intended for men? Do the women who smoke 'Marlboro' really want to be men? Not at all. There is no threat to their femininity, because the advertisement symbolises not merely maleness, but everything that goes with it—power, status, success and confidence. Marlboro were, in fact, originally marketed by Philip Morris in the 1920s as a brand with a strong *female* image, carrying the slogan, 'Cherry tips to match your ruby lips' (the cigarette tips were red). The brand failed dismally. Philip Morris allowed the female association to fade, and re-launched the brand with the Marlboro cowboy in 1955. Marlboro now sells more cigarettes than any other brand in the world.

Strategy No. 2: the Sex-Impartial Attack

The advertisers who used to portray cigarettes as a symbol of male strength now incorporate female strength into them as well. There has been a transition from the ultra-virile male who stared out from billboards telling you to smoke the masculine smoke, to a new approach in which as many women as men tell us to 'Taste Winston Lights' or that 'Now' cigarettes are a 'satisfying decision'. The women are serious decision-makers: 'I made a decision about low tar,' says the 'Vantage' lady solemnly. Indeed, some of the adverts go in for what could almost be described as role-reversal—other Vantage ads show him lighting *her* cigarette, while he doesn't smoke. Benson & Hedges go a step further, depicting a woman who is so emancipated that she smokes *and* puts a protective arm around her man. Although sexual innuendo is played down in advertisements aimed at both men and women, there is the familiar enticing female pout in Kent ads. In the Salem series, 'he' is depicted in strong determined profile while 'she' is represented as a pair of neon-red lips, slightly parted. There is also the curious aproned lady whom you would expect to recommend the product with a demureness befitting her wifely appearance. Instead, she looks you straight in the eye and says assertively: 'I want the best taste I can get.'

Strategy No. 3: the Female Cigarette

To label a cigarette as female means that you cut out your male market. It is possible to thrive on selling a male image to women, but it simply will not do for a man to be seen smoking a cigarette designed for ladies.

Hoping to ride the crest of the 1960s wave of liberation, Liggett & Myers—one of the largest companies in the US—launched 'Eve' which bade 'Farewell to the ugly cigarette . . . Smoke pretty Eve—a cigarette as feminine as the ring you wear.' The cigarettes themselves came complete with flowery pack and filter. But L & M had misread the signs of the times and women had already begun to move away from their traditional preoccupations. Eve was a failure. Other brands similarly directed at creating the glamorous sexy-lady image did not do well either: ads for 'Silva Thins', for instance, showing a beautiful woman explaining why she is a 'Thinner', fell on barren ground, along with ads for 'Max', another cigarette directed exclusively at women. Out of the failure grew a more effective approach, creating the impression that a female cigarette had become essential equipment for gaining equality in a man's world.

First to use this theme was 'Virginia Slims', masterminded by Philip Morris who launched their product at exactly the right time—1968. Feminism was gathering momentum, and, as cigarette advertising had not yet been banned on TV, it did much to boost sales. The advertising agency responsible for the campaign knew what was at stake: 'You are competing with every other advertiser for a share of the consumer's mind,' it said.[8] And so Philip Morris went after women with their slogan, 'You've come a long way, baby.'

The early Virginia Slims girls were depicted as slightly coy and giggly, but Philip Morris' confidence soared along with sales. Today's ads are hard-hitting and aggressive, usually comparing the poor oppressed wives of the past with today's jet-setter or woman executive. But the magazine and billboard ads are only part of the advertising jamboree. Women can now themselves become walking cigarette ads with Philip Morris' special offers of 'Ginny' jump jackets or sports shorts. Virginia Slims even sponsored a major art exhibition on women through the ages, as well as the first widely-publicised women's opinion poll. By 1976 Virginia Slims had become *the* women's cigarette, ranking as the fifteenth best-selling brand in the US and selling enough cigarettes to keep half-a-million women smoking a pack a day.[9,10] A basic annual budget of $8 million and sales rising steadily at about seven per cent a year—[11] even the advertisers have admitted that the success of the Virginia Slims campaign has 'surpassed all our fantasies'.

The Virginia Slims girl may have come a long way, but she is still someone's 'baby'. She's only playing at being the independent woman. It's suggested that her cigarettes are her passport to slimness because they are 'Slimmer than the fat cigarettes men smoke'. By appealing to women in two conflicting ways, the campaign captures both the strengths *and* the vulnerabilities of women and sells them nearly nine billion cigarettes every year.[12]

10. British Cunning

British cigarette advertising, worth nearly £100 million a year,[1] seems relatively benign—at first. It is certainly less overtly hard-line than the American approach. But it would be misleading to judge the British tobacco companies' tactics by current advertisements alone, because to a considerable extent they reflect the response of an industry forced by government to modify the content of its advertising.

The British Way of Selling

Given governmental constraints on advertising, British manufacturers have been less able to aim for specific target groups such as women and have invested increasing amounts of money into more general strategies aimed, instead, at the whole population. Despite two major reports from the Royal College of Physicians calling for legislation to ban cigarette advertising,[2,3] advertisements for cigarettes such as Slim Kings—which appeared in the early 1970s, after the second report—still promised sex, sophistication and elegance.

Until the early 1970s, the '*macho*' line of attack was popular in Britain. The virile Marlboro cowboy characterised this theme with the world-renowned slogan, 'Come to Marlboro Country—come to where the flavour is.' Close behind was the thoroughly British and commercially successful Rothmans pilot whose job it was to persuade you to smoke Rothmans, 'When you know what you're doing.' Anxious to test the British female public, the American companies tried to launch an all-female cigarette, but women were not impressed by 'long, luxurious Silva Thins' and remained remarkably loyal to their usual British brands. Reyno Menthol, another American brand, also tried to cash in by offering women a calorie counter, while suggesting that 'Reyno Menthol helps the inches go.' But the Advertising Standards Authority—the watchdog of British print advertising—would not accept this theme on the grounds that it made misleading claims that its product aided slimming, and Reyno was forced to withdraw it. Companies such as John Player stepped up the more subtle, but nonetheless effective British flirtation with themes of feminine elegance. Advertisements for John Player Special conjured up images of wealth and female sophistication with the slogan: 'Shoes by Yves St Laurent. Cigarettes by John Player.' The advertisements juxtaposed a pair of carelessly discarded, black, diamond-studded evening shoes and the shimmering black-and-gold John Player Special pack. But by 1975, campaigners at ASH, the anti-smoking pressure group, had begun making life difficult for the cigarette companies.

Following a series of complaints about cigarette advertising as a whole, ASH persuaded the Advertising Standards Authority (ASA) to adopt a special code of advertising practice for cigarettes, which meant that all advertisements in the printed media had to be approved by ASA before publication. The new code required that advertisements:

> should not seek to encourage people, particularly the young, to start smoking or, if they are already smokers, to increase their level of smoking or smoke to excess; and should not exploit those who are especially vulnerable.[4]

In particular, the code specified that advertisements were no longer allowed to suggest that smoking was 'a sign or proof of manliness, or that smokers were more virile or tough than non-smokers'. The clause meant goodbye to the Marlboro cowboy and the Rothmans pilot. But what ASH forgot was that there was nothing to stop the advertisements appealing to femininity. So the associations between smoking, femininity and elegance continued. Despite a further clause in the code, which stated that advertisements 'should not seek directly or indirectly to establish either that smoking is socially advantageous, particularly sophisticated, smart, up-to-date or associated with a luxurious way of life', the elegance of ladies who smoked St Moritz slipped into such magazines as *Cosmopolitan* with the greatest of ease. In theory, the St Moritz ad broke at least four rules in the ASA code—especially the rule requiring that advertisements 'should not appear in any publication directed wholly or mainly to young people',[5] for the bulk of *Cosmopolitan*'s readership is young. The difficulty with this voluntary code, however, is that discretion on its application lies solely with the ASA—a purportedly impartial body, set up by the advertising industry which is itself heavily represented on ASA committees.

Following the failure of the aggressively feminine approach,

British manufacturers opted, like the Americans, for a safe, sex-impartial attack: safe because it is an approach that slips easily through the ASA code and safe, too, because it does not risk losing male smokers. Most took the simplest available course, extending the hitherto male images of their brands to include female versions without changing the slogans. Attractive young women slowly began to appear alongside the young men who laughed out from bill-boards proclaiming 'People like you are changing to No. 6.' Blonde women, dark women, middle-class women, not-so-middle-class women and even older women appeared in the No. 6 series, on their own or together with their male counterparts. In the mid-1970s there was a subtle change to an emphasis on women rather than men, but today they have returned to reassuring both sexes that the lower-tar versions of their brands make a good 'egalitarian' smoke. Other advertisers caught on more slowly, but the luxurious scenes portraying 'The World of Lambert & Butler' changed subtly, almost imperceptibly. They remained broadly similar in style, but the elegant non-smoking women who used to look on from the periphery began to smoke alongside their equally chic male partners.

Low Tar—the 'Mild' Smoke

It has not escaped the notice of the British manufacturers that women, particularly, can easily be persuaded to smoke low-tar cigarettes. In Britain, as in the US, growing anti-smoking pressure forced the manufacturers to produce new lower-tar cigarettes, but the incentive to go all out for low-tar cigarettes has been even stronger in Britain because of the increased tax on high-tar cigarettes. The new Embassy Extra Mild—launched in the late-1970s—went one stage further in enticing female customers: it offered a kitchen diary-planner in return for five of the new pack-fronts. No. 6 Extra Mild, on the other hand, backed up its advertising campaign with an exclusive offer to *Woman* and *Woman's Own* readers of a free copy of *The Golden Hands Book of Dressmaking Patterns*. Thus UK advertisers, too, have lulled women into a false sense of low-tar security, and more women of all ages and social groups now smoke low-tar cigarettes, the most receptive being young, middle-class women.[6]

The Female Cigarette that Had to Go

In 1976, Philip Morris, still dizzy from its successful launch of

Virginia Slims in the US, decided to try to lure British women into the Virginia Slims habit. In the interests of British female sensitivities, they used a different blend of tobacco, and even modified the sexist 'Baby' slogan which had so offended *Ms* magazine. October 1976 saw the aggressive £2 million launch of the anglicised version of Virginia Slims with the slogan, 'We've come a long, long way.' The theme of the woman who discovers her emancipation through her cigarettes is otherwise the same as the American version.

ASH was incensed. It was the first overt attempt in Britain to use women's liberation to sell cigarettes, Mike Daube, then director of ASH, protested immediately to the ASA. 'The ads deliberately attempt to exploit the women's movement and are thus trying to recruit new smokers,' he said. 'The Virginia Slims advertisements are directed at a specific sector of the market where there is still room for expansion.' Despite appearing to break nearly every rule in the ASA code, the ASA was unable, at the time, to see 'how the campaign could be said to seek to persuade women to start smoking'. It did, however, express 'considerable reservations' about the adverts, which it saw as being 'in doubtful taste because they exploited the campaign for women's rights'. However, finding the ads objectionable on these grounds was not sufficient reason to reject them, explained the ASA, because there was no clause in the cigarette code which prevented Philip Morris from pursuing its line.

Not satisfied with plastering hoardings, magazines and newspapers, Philip Morris approached the editor of *Ms London*, a magazine aimed mainly at working women aged between 16 and 24, who agreed to let them use the magazine to run a competition. All readers had to do was answer some questions about such 'female revolutionaries' as Princess Anne, and complete the slogan: 'Virginia Slims are perfect for the modern woman because . . . .' The six best entrants won prizes which included an elegant pen and propelling pencil set.[7] The incident provoked immediate parliamentary questions from two MPs, Laurie Pavitt and Lynda Chalker, and a sharp condemnation from the then Health Minister, Roland Moyle, who was concerned that the ASA did not consider the *Ms London* ploy in breach of the cigarette code: 'This strengthens our view . . . that the present [ASA] Code does not go far enough.'[8] It is ironic that this first official parliamentary recognition of the growing smoking problem in women was prompted by a tobacco company's own efforts to sell cigarettes. When the ASA code was revised in 1977, ASH made sure that, alongside the virility clause, there was an equivalent femininity clause which, theoretically at least, protected women against any similar future adverts. Today, advertisements are not allowed to suggest that 'female smokers are more glamorous or independent than non-smokers' or that 'smoking enhances feminine charm.'[9]

The Cut-Price Trap

The cut-price game is a particularly effective way of persuading housewives, and anyone else who can ill-afford cigarettes, to buy more cigarettes. The supermarket is still a predominantly female arena and an ideal place to catch women under thirty.[10] Teenagers and housewives now spend more than three times as much on cigarettes as on confectionery, and one-and-a-half times as much as on cosmetics.[11] The importance of the supermarket as a retail outlet has not escaped the attention of the tobacco companies, as an executive of Wills Tobacco Company recently confirmed, 'because of the recognition of the importance of the female smoker.'[12] The Co-op chain of food-stores (so popular in the north of England where lung cancer rates are among the highest) estimate that their cigarette sales could soon reach £50 million a year—[13]enough to keep two-and-a-half million women smoking 20 cigarettes a day. In the US, 45 per cent of total cigarette sales are now from supermarkets.[14]

As supermarket shoppers buy up to half their purchases on impulse,[15] the supermarket is an extremely effective place in which to promote cigarettes. If you were to ask housewives what kind of product incentives they prefer, they would probably say price-cuts, free samples and coupons, in that order.[16] The cigarette companies offer all of them. This makes sense, especially since there is evidence that women are more sensitive to the price of cigarettes than are men—the lower the price, the more likely women are to buy cigarettes.[17] It comes as no surprise, therefore, to learn that sales of cut-price cigarettes flourish in supermarkets. Tesco, for example, has an agreement with the Gallaher Tobacco Company to set up kiosks selling cut-price cigarettes, which are intended to attract customers to items for sale nearby in the shop.

Lung Cancer and Other Free Gifts

Collecting gift coupons has, until relatively recently, been one of the hallmarks of British smoking practice. Following the ban on TV advertising in 1965, the tobacco companies increased their expenditure on cigarette gift-coupon schemes from £8 million to as much as £24 million. By 1975, it had reached an all-time high of £50 million—the industry's single biggest advertising investment.[18] Coupons, with their illusion of offering something for nothing, were an ideal way of keeping people smoking, and smoking more, and provided an added incentive to postpone the decision to stop. Women, especially housewives, are an obvious and lucrative target. Take Tanya, who is 29, married and has two children. Her attitude to cigarette coupons is fairly typical: 'Sometimes I used to buy more cigarettes than I really wanted, because I needed another hundred coupons towards something I wanted to get out of the gift catalogue.' Tanya doesn't collect coupons anymore, but she can't stop smoking either.

Spot the Kensitas Smoker . . .

The cigarette gift catalogues, like the Green Shield stamp catalogues, speak primarily to women. The message to the woman-smoker from the 1978 Kensitas gift catalogue was: 'There's something for every member of the family.' If she smoked twenty cigarettes a day for thirty years—the average time it takes to develop lung cancer—she could collect an electric sewing machine, along with a cot and mattress for her baby. 'You get more out of life with a Kensitas,' said the ads. Kensitas people were usually young. They were beautiful. And they whiled away their time sailing luxurious boats in which the women relaxed with a Kensitas. They also shared moonlit barbecues where men and women smoked Kensitas. But Kensitas had something else to offer; with ten coupons per pack, you could 'get your gift twice as fast'. The ads went on to explain, with unwitting accuracy, that with cigarettes, as with other things, 'you get out of life what you put into it.' When ASH pointed out that what you get is lung cancer, heart disease and bronchitis, Kensitas withdrew the ad series. More recent advertisements changed their emphasis. 'Can you spot the Kensitas smoker?', they asked. She was the housewife with the electric food-mixer (thanks to Kensitas) and a self-satisfied smirk. The non-smoking housewives who flanked her, struggling with the 'impossible' task of manual food-mixing, were harassed, sweaty and incompetent by contrast.

Today's Tactics

Although the ASA code has forced tobacco companies to move to more surreal, even extraterrestrial themes in advertising, evidence of ASA's peculiar brand of impartiality comes from the process by which the old 'macho' and feminine glamour themes have crept back into the ads. Following the Marlboro cowboy's demise in 1975, Philip Morris had to think again. Their subsequent ads portrayed cowboy country and cowboy paraphernalia, but no cowboys. But the loopholes in the ASA code—always open to interpretation—along with some ingenuity on the part of Philip Morris' advertising agency, soon resurrected the ghost of the cowboy. Today's Marlboro man appears in soft focus, with a late-seventies unisex appeal.

The sex-impartial Player's No. 6 images of a few years back have also been superseded by similar adverts which slip through the ASA code. Today's advertisements portray the successful, sophisticated career woman (or man) assuring you that part of being clever, attractive and successful is smoking John Player King Size. The ads seemed to break the femininity as well as other clauses of the code, but, when challenged, the ASA seemed more interested in dabbling in semantics than in confronting the real intentions behind the advertising. ASA director, Peter Thompson, said: 'This advertisement may suggest that some charming women smoke, but I don't think it suggests that anybody becomes charming by smoking.' Some of today's cigarette advertisements may *appear* less sexist than a few years ago, but the thinking behind them remains unchanged.

11. The Health Educators

Most of us can remember the first anti-smoking TV commercials, intended to shake us into giving up smoking. The UK commercials likened smokers to lemmings who hurled themselves off cliffs to certain death. In the US, William Talman, Perry Mason's well-loved but heavy-smoking judicial opponent, told millions of American viewers, simply and dramatically: 'I have lung cancer.' He died before the commercials came on the air. These shock/

horror tactics certainly had an immediate impact. Following the first of an impressive series of 'This Week' documentaries on smoking, which told the story of a 42-year-old man dying of lung cancer, a Gallup Poll showed that the programme had prompted 160,000 smokers to give up. But women did not figure independently in any of the early health-education campaigns. The health educators intended their message for all smokers, but the major response, as we have already seen, was from men.

The Evolution of the 'Skin-Deep Sinner'

Women later became the focus of anti-smoking fervour—as wives and mothers. The *British Medical Journal* described the woman-smoker as 'imposing a threat to her procreative role'.[1] 'The young mother who smokes', according to the *Journal of the Royal College of General Practitioners*, 'is throwing away her child's birthright by increasing its chances of death and malnutrition'.[2]

If women were not moved by their responsibilities as mothers, a *Daily Mail* medical correspondent advised them on 'twenty ways to help your husband avoid a heart attack', one of which was stopping smoking.[3] The Department of Education had another method of reaching schoolgirls, most of whom would one day become wives. It advised teachers running anti-smoking programmes to enlist the help of the girls in their efforts to persuade the boys to stop smoking. The department had not, apparently, recognised what 13-year-old Mark told a *Daily Mail* reporter at the time: 'It's no good the government thinking we can be influenced by the girls; doesn't it know that the girls are smoking too?'[4] And ultimately, of course, the women who would not be moved by their feminine duties, could, according to the campaigners, be persuaded only by the one remaining approach—sex. If a woman could be convinced that smoking might ruin her chances of getting a man, that surely would make her stop.

Thus newspapers claimed that smoking is one of the 'seven deadly sins of woman', causing, for instance, premature wrinkles —a conclusion based on evidence from one doctor in California who assessed the severity of the 'crow's feet' which developed in four-hundred smokers compared with non-smokers.[5] 'After all, what woman wants to look twenty years older than she is?', asks Dr Alfred Yarrow, writing in the British Medical Association's *Family Doctor* booklet on smoking.[6] The media find it hard to take the woman smoker seriously. At the first ASH conference devoted to women and smoking in 1975, newspaper reporters seemed fixated on one message: 'Smoked out, girls?', read a typical headline in the *Daily Express*, 'Sex is better for you.'[7]

Receptacles for the Next Generation

The philosophy behind these health-education approaches is a reflection of society's view of men and women—that men will always be men, but women can only be wives, mothers or sex objects. The underlying assumption is that a woman's motives for doing anything are always to satisfy others. She must, therefore, stop smoking to protect her unborn child, her husband or her sex appeal. The messages directed at women depend largely on generating sufficient guilt and anxiety to make her stop. Thus health educators reinforce ideas about the proper way for women to behave. So far their tactics have done little more than undermine the self-confidence of the woman who is trying to stay off cigarettes.

Britain's Perfect Non-Smoking Mum

In 1973, Alastair Mackie, then newly-appointed director of the Health Education Council (HEC), felt it was time to capitalise on the accumulating evidence that smoking could damage the unborn child. Unlike his counterparts at the Scottish Health Education Unit (SHEU) whose primary campaigns deliberately avoided using shocking images because of what SHEU described as 'a delicate psychological situation',[8] Alastair Mackie was a strong advocate of using as controversial an approach as possible.

The first poster series for the HEC smoking-in-pregnancy campaign certainly lived up to his philosophy. It featured a nude pregnant woman against the bold caption: 'Is it fair to force your baby to smoke cigarettes?' In the accompanying TV commercial showing a tiny under-weight baby in an incubator, the medical voice of doom warned: 'You may deprive your baby of oxygen . . . you may poison its bloodstream with nicotine . . . it may even threaten his life.' The campaign cost £160,000 and soaked up nearly two-thirds of the HEC's anti-smoking budget for the year.[9] With two further campaigns, expenditure intended to cut smoking in pregnancy—£500,000 by 1978—came to more than 20 per cent of the smoking and health budget since 1972.

Can this campaign be justified? Did it achieve its two stated aims of reducing smoking in pregnancy and alerting all women to the dangers of smoking? Alastair Mackie maintains that it did because a survey commissioned by the HEC before and after the 1973 campaign showed that the proportion of smokers among pregnant women fell from 39 per cent to 29 per cent.[10] But did the campaign cause the fall? It is impossible to say, because the survey did not compare those who watched the adverts with a control group of pregnant women who were not aware of the campaign. And similar research into the effects of later campaigns showed no overall impact on pregnant women. In fact, research funded by the HEC itself shows that 15 per cent of women spontaneously stop smoking when they first become pregnant.[11]

Why was it necessary to use a nude model? In a letter to the *British Medical Journal* at the time, Alastair Mackie claimed that 'a lot of research established quite clearly that the naked woman would bring home the simple medical points . . . far more effectively than an anatomical diagram'. The research, which was never published, was based on the reactions of nine women attending one session of an ante-natal clinic.[12] Before the nude was adopted, the HEC commissioned a pilot study of four different approaches to combating smoking in pregnancy. The study, which involved 90 women, did not show the nude model, only the caption (with a clothed model) which eventually accompanied it.[13] Alastair Mackie explained that the nude emerged later out of a conversation he had with his chief medical officer: 'I can remember thinking in a crude way what a tremendous topic this was for public relations work.' Looking back on the campaign, he admits that the decision-making process was inherently sexist: 'The vast majority of people involved in the work [the publicity officer, chief medical officer, advertising copy writer] were men, so you've got inbuilt sexism—albeit unconscious.'

A Misdirected Campaign

Let us assume that such campaigns do persuade some pregnant women to stop smoking. Are they justified? There are, on average, just over half-a-million women in England and Wales each year who are either pregnant or thinking of becoming so. Assuming four in ten pregnant women smoke, the total target audience for the campaign is 200,000 female smokers out of a possible total of nine million women smokers. By comparison, there are about three million women who take the pill and are doubly at risk from the combined effects of the pill and cigarettes. Yet the HEC has been silent on this front.

Can the medical evidence alone justify directing the *entire* female anti-smoking effort towards smoking in pregnancy? Alastair Mackie says yes, although the grounds accepted by the HEC were challenged at the time and were never formally published. There can be no doubt that smoking in pregnancy *can* damage the unborn child, but the risk to the child is *far smaller* than the risk the women herself is taking. The pregnant woman who smokes heavily is less than twice as likely as a non-smoker to lose her baby at or near birth—[14],[15] a small risk compared with the five-times greater likelihood she herself faces of developing lung cancer compared with a non-smoker.[16] So, on statistical grounds alone, it is hard to avoid the conclusion that the money spent on mass-media campaigns against smoking in pregnancy were largely misguided. The emotional slogans are even harder to justify. The warning given in the TV commercial that women who smoke while pregnant may give birth to babies with 'thin arms and wasted flesh' is based on evidence that pregnant women who smoke give birth to babies who are, *on average*, 6oz lighter than those born to non-smokers. But, *smoking may not be the most important risk to a baby's health*: the risk factor varies enormously with who you are and how you live. If you are young, white, well-nourished and smoke fewer than ten cigarettes a day, the extra risk of 'killing your baby' is no more than ten per cent above that of a white non-smoker. By contrast, the black woman who smokes heavily is twice as likely to lose her baby as a black non-smoker.[17]

Could the campaign even have done more harm than good? It was intended to make women respond by making them feel guilty. Many obliged—but few actually stopped smoking, which made them feel even more guilty. And a campaign that concentrates on pregnancy may make women assume it's all right to smoke *unless* they are pregnant, thus leading many to postpone stopping *until* they are pregnant.

Follow My Leader

Once it was accepted that the way to approach a woman smoker was through her children, other countries such as France, Australia and Canada followed suit. The American Cancer Society's (ACS) approach has been the one exception. Recognising the potential for appealing to women in the interests of their *own* health, the ACS has launched a new series of campaigns directed at women. Early versions used the black actress Lola

Falana, who tantalised her viewers with her non-smoking glamour. More recently, the ACS launched an initiative directed at women as part of its ambitious five-year programme to reduce cigarette smoking.[18] And for the first time in the history of the anti-smoking campaign, the American Cancer Society produced a film featuring a *woman* smoker who had developed lung cancer. Moreover, the US Department of Health, Education and Welfare followed the ACS example and produced publicity material in which ill-health in women themselves figured as prominently as the dangers of smoking in pregnancy.

Meanwhile, the Health Education Council continues—with few exceptions—to base its campaigns on the idea that a woman's goal in life is to nurture her husband and children. A £300,000 campaign launched at the end of 1979 used TV commercials in which young boys and girls played 'mummies and daddies'. 'Daddy' comes home from work and looks for his cigarettes while 'mummy' gives him a cup of tea and warns him 'not in front of the children', gesticulating towards the dolls. 'Daddy' pays no attention and inhales a crayon. It seems to have escaped the Health Education Council's notice that times, and roles, have changed.

12. The Political Activists

A Conspicuous Absence

The absence of women at all levels of the anti-smoking campaign is equalled only by the lack of priority campaigners have given to the problem of smoking among women.

At the first World Conference on Smoking and Health in 1967, only three speakers out of fifty were women. The specific problems of women smokers were not raised at all.[1] The third World Conference was held in 1975, and a sub-section entitled 'women and cigarettes' appeared for the first time, largely as a concession to International Woman's Year. But once the year was over, the problem was soon forgotten. June 1979 saw the fourth gathering of the international anti-smoking experts and, of sixty major speakers, only ten were women. The only paper on women

74

was given by a man, Julian Peto, a medical statistician who admitted to me at the time that smoking was no longer his field of expertise. The level of concern about smoking among women was aptly summed up by Mike Daube, former director of ASH and now a World Health Organisation (WHO) consultant: 'The smoking-and-health campaign has been run by middle-class, middle-aged men, and it is middle-class, middle-aged men who have given up [smoking] . . . perhaps the smoking-and-health campaign needs to change itself while it seeks to change others.'[2]

For many many years, WHO has taken a firm stand on smoking and health, and has produced three major reports with strong recommendations to member governments for smoking controls. The first, in 1971, by two eminent male anti-smoking campaigners, expressed no particular thoughts on women.[3] The second, in 1975, compiled by a committee of nine men, reiterated the now familiar view that women who smoked jeopardised their children's health.[4] By 1979, when female lung-cancer rates were soaring in the more developed countries, WHO made a gesture unique in the history of smoking and health, and included one woman on its second expert Committee on Smoking. This, it emerges, was because two of its members insisted that it would have been embarrassing not to include at least one woman. By early 1980, WHO apparently felt it was time to initiate a campaign directed at women, but several months later abandoned its plans.

American Activists

Luther Terry, the then US Surgeon General, masterminded the first major American report on smoking and health, published in 1964. There were nine men on the committee that compiled it, and it dealt with women mainly under the section entitled 'Other conditions'[5] which included preliminary findings on the effects of smoking on the unborn child. Looking back at the early days of the campaign, Luther Terry admitted to me: 'We didn't really consider the problem in women then.'

Women continued to be ignored in the Surgeon General's reports on smoking until 1973, when a section on smoking in pregnancy appeared.[6] The problems of the woman smoker herself were not publicly recognised until after the publication of the 1979 report. This was the first of its kind to review some of the evidence for sex differences in smoking trends. But more importantly, it gave official credence to the rumours accumulating over the years

75

that women find it harder to stop smoking than do men.[7] Joseph Califano, then US Secretary of Health, Education and Welfare, was the main impetus behind the move, and before President Carter sacked him for what were considered to be excessive anti-smoking views, Califano did much for the cause. Indeed, the Tobacco Institute, the collective voice of the tobacco industry, became so worried by the potential reduction in the female market that it produced a detailed 'rebuttal' of the growing claims that smoking could damage a woman's health, even rejecting the evidence that smoking causes lung cancer![8]

Califano perceptively pointed out that 'cigarettes may hold a more addictive power over women than men,'[9] and was responsible for the decision to devote the entire 1980 Surgeon General's report to women. But he still behaved very much like other male campaigners before him. In his public pronouncements he seemed more anxious to protect the health of the foetus than that of the child's mother. 'Before you take up a habit that is so hard to give up', he said in an appeal to women in April 1979, 'think about the baby you may someday have.'[10]

The British Campaigners

In 1962, the Royal College of Physicians shattered the world of the smoker with its initial report on the effects of cigarettes.[11] Compiled by a committee of nine men, the report set out to summarise the evidence of the deleterious effects of smoking on health, and made recommendations to government and other bodies on reducing cigarette consumption. We can forgive the Royal College for its cursory reference to women smokers, as the report was published before data on women was available. But by 1977, when its third report was published, there was little sign of progress. Although the committee that compiled it contained twice as many members as the 1962 committee, there were no women on it. It is also an interesting reflection on the lack of British commitment to the smoking problem in women that the report had to borrow American statistics on smoking and lung cancer in women because equivalent British figures did not exist.[12] But the report did devote a chapter to smoking in pregnancy.[13] By contrast with similar American reports, there were no references to evidence indicating sex differences in motivation to smoke and in ability to stop.

A spokesman from the Department of Health reminded me

that 'smoking is as hazardous in men as it is in women,' and stated that government could not be expected to 'restrict its attempts to reduce smoking to any particular group'—although he admitted that the young got special attention. Sir George Young, Health Minister with responsibility for smoking-and-health policy, made no reference to the incidence of lung cancer in women in his otherwise hard-hitting address at the fourth World Conference on Smoking in Stockholm. Yet he later justified his refusal to grant me an interview on this subject on the grounds that he doubted whether he could *add* anything to what he had already said. Asked by Laurie Pavitt MP, who formerly chaired the House of Commons All-Party Group for Action on Smoking and Health, whether he was prepared to hold a departmental inquiry into smoking and the ill-health it caused in women, Sir George refused.[14]

It has not proved any easier to persuade parliament to take the issue seriously. The 1977 report from the House of Commons Sub-committee on Preventive Medicine was chaired by Renée Short, Labour MP for Wolverhampton North East. One of its ten recommendations was that the government should devote considerable attention to the problem of weight-gain as a barrier to stopping smoking.[15] This committee was the first to make a recommendation of direct importance to the woman smoker and the first major committee to be chaired by a woman. But like many of the other women's-health problems that Renée Short has raised in parliament, the matter ended there. Her committee's recommendations were largely ignored. As she says:

> It matters little whether the government is labour or tory, it is virtually impossible to get any issue related to women's health raised in a place like this [parliament]. You can take great pains to draw the minister's attention to the increasing number of women suffering from lung cancer, but all you get in return is fine words—never any action.

Perhaps the priority given by politicians to the smoking problem among women is best illustrated by a debate in the House of Lords in 1979 in which Lord Airedale asked the government speaker why—in the face of increasing smoking rates among women—no anti-smoking campaigns were being directed specifically at women. Lord Leatherland, backed by Lord Cullen, the government speaker on health, felt that such a campaign would be counter-productive, because, in his opinion, women 'may resort to other vices which are less acceptable.'[16]

The Silence of the Women's Movement

A peculiar silence—almost a resistance—surrounds the question of smoking among women's organisations. As far as the women's movement is concerned, smoking is someone else's problem. The now prolific literature on women's health and health care is remarkable for lack of attention to the issue. *Our Bodies Ourselves*, for instance, is an indispensable health handbook for women, published in British and American editions. The British edition has only one passing, and dismissive, reference to smoking.[17] Judy Norsigian, a member of the Boston Women's Health Collective which produced the original US edition of the book, explained that they had intended including a chapter on smoking, alcohol and drugs but 'there was not sufficient room in the book, and we did not have the resources to do the research.'

I contacted more than fifty women's organisations on both sides of the Atlantic, some feminist, some not, some national and some local, but most failed to reply. The National Organisation of Women (NOW), for instance, which has taken a highly active role on many women's health issues in the USA, was not prepared to comment, and in its 40-page submission to the 1979 Kennedy hearings on women's health, NOW did not make a single reference to the problem.[18] Indeed, had the American Cancer Society not referred to the rising lung-cancer rates in women in its own evidence to the hearings, the issue would not have been raised at all.

The National Women's Health Network, which represents over a thousand American women's health organisations, has 'no formal position on smoking'. The National Women's Political Caucus, well-known for its firm stance on such issues as abortion and contraception, considered smoking to be 'neither a national nor a legislative issue', and thus 'have no policy' on smoking: 'Smoking', they said, 'is a general concern; our role is to concentrate on those health concerns which are specific to women.' Replies from local groups were similar. The San Francisco Women's Health Collective, an organisation which describes itself as devoted to 'women's health education', had not discussed smoking because 'it was not a priority in terms of health education'. The response from the Berkeley Women's Health Collective was the same.

It is the same story in Britain. At the London-based Women's Research and Resources Centre there was no record of any work or research on the subject, and most of the organisations

78

I approached did not reply. Although a few MPs have raised the issue sporadically in parliament, there have been no specific initiatives from women's organisations. The 1979 Conference of Labour Women went so far as to ban smoking at its meetings, but while it passed strong resolutions recommending action on other women's health issues ranging from abortion and cervical cancer to home deliveries and dental infections, there was no similar resolution on smoking and health. The response from a wide range of other women's organisations has been no more encouraging. The management committee of the National Council of Women, which represents more than a hundred women's societies, felt that 'other organisations should do the job'; and the Women's National Cancer Control Campaign, an active promoter of preventive policies to deal with cervical and breast cancers, felt the same. Prevention of smoking, they explained, could only become a major part of their work if 'research were to point to a connection between smoking and one of the forms of cancer with which we are involved'.

Many local feminist and therapy groups expressed an interest in the problem, but were reluctant to commit time to it. The Women's Therapy Centre in London thought it would be 'terrific' if feminists started groups for women trying to stop smoking, but felt that their organisation 'couldn't offer anything'. The Birmingham Women's Health Group seemed to sum up the prevailing attitude among many British women's groups:

> When we read your letter there was a great reluctance in the group to spend a whole meeting discussing smoking. Most members (despite being smokers themselves) felt there were more important issues to discuss.

What Does the Silence Mean?

Smoking is a major and growing health problem for women. So how can feminists stand by while the tobacco industry exploits women, and health educators respond with inept propaganda? The reasons for this silence seem to stem largely from the evolution of the women's movement itself.

Campaigns about women's reproductive health such as the fight for abortion and contraception, have long been political cornerstones of the women's movement. Yet the early campaigns were not based primarily on health considerations,[19] but on the economic consequences of ill-health and unwanted pregnancies.

It was not until the growth of feminism in the sixties that

79

a woman's health movement developed in its own right. The relative affluence of the period allowed women, for the first time, to approach the question of health from a very different standpoint. Thus women were able to pay much more attention to the basic quality of their lives, and to explore the broader meaning of health and the ways in which a sexist society generates ill-health among women. Contraception and abortion remained an integral part of the women's health movement, but the emphasis changed. Following legislation extending the availability of abortion, and the widespread use of the pill, women became primarily concerned with the health and safety implications of existing methods of fertility control. The new interest in health spread. Women re-wrote the psychology books, campaigned against those who 'tranquillised' their spirits, and began to explore the realms of alternative medicine.

Breast cancer and cancer of the cervix (the neck of the womb) have become concerns of the women's movement, but smoking and other equally pressing problems such as alcoholism have not. This is not just because women believe that they are largely male problems, but also because women are reacting against society and the medical profession which exhorts us not to smoke—for our children's sake. The long-standing libertarian tradition of feminism tends to view anti-smoking campaigns as yet another manifestation of male 'experts' telling women what they can or can't do with their bodies. But the main reason is that women's organisations still see their priorities in the terms their sisters did earlier this century. At that time, an almost total lack of political and legal rights, superimposed on economic hardship, forced women to concentrate on reproductive issues. But today the climate is different. Western women rarely die in childbirth, and the birthrate has been falling. Although the right to safe fertility control is still vital, health isues for women have spread beyond the genitals. Many women now argue that, in the face of new threats to our reproductive rights, smoking can only be of secondary importance. But it is dangerous to justify one priority by ignoring another. It is as urgent to deal with smoking, which kills and maims more women than breast and cervical cancers combined, as it is to fight for improved contraception and abortion facilities. There is surely room within the women's movement to use the proven strength of women's groups to tackle the smoking problem, as well as other women's health issues.

II. Helping Yourself

13. Thinking About Stopping?

Telling people why they should stop smoking is the easiest thing in the world. You have heard anti-smoking campaigners doing it for nearly two decades and you probably agree with what they say. Yet you still find you can't stop. Other people around you seem to have managed without much hardship. How did they do it? 'Sheer strength of character,' they say infuriatingly. Your doctor has probably told you it's all a question of willpower—'as easy as throwing your last pack of cigarettes in the bin,' Tanya's GP told her. But that didn't anwer Tanya's question—she wanted to know how to cope with the craving. 'Run round the block when you get the urge to smoke,' he offered helpfully. 'I suppose he expected me to run round the bloody block 60 times a day,' said Tanya.

Nobody will tell you how to find that elusive willpower, or how to hang on to it—least of all the experts. It's all very well for anti-smoking enthusiasts to describe smoking as the 'largest avoidable hazard to health'; but to you it's just one of the many problems you have to cope with. You may not want to join the 50,000 British smokers who die prematurely, but it seems pointless to lie awake at night agonising about it. The key to dealing with your smoking problem is to make it number one priority in your life—for a short while at least. The first step towards solving any problem is concentrating on it.

In the following chapters I hope to help you focus your attention on smoking and the part it plays in your life. Then I'll give you a framework for stopping. There is no single, miraculous cure for smoking; and despite what many people say, they key lies not so much in the method itself as in how you approach the problem.

The Four Key Questions

If giving up smoking were simply a matter of acknowledging its dangers, you would probably have stopped a long time ago. Some smokers simply clicked their fingers and stopped when they first heard about the risks. But you are still smoking today—despite knowing the dangers. So it is important that, before you throw away your last pack, you make sure you are quite clear about what is at stake. There are four **key questions** you must answer before you try to stop smoking and you will not be successful until you are clear about the answers.

1. **Why should I stop?** If you haven't got a good enough reason you won't stop. Other people's reasons may not be yours.

2. **Will I get more out of giving up than continuing to smoke?** All the official publicity tells how bad smoking is for you. But you know that you get something out of smoking. What is it? How important is it for you to smoke? What do you see as the benefits of stopping? The woman who has had a heart attack may feel she has more to gain than the woman who has not yet suffered any ill effects of smoking. Are you prepared to risk becoming ill?

3. **Have I the confidence to stop?** Giving up, as we have seen, is not just a matter of reason and motivation, but also depends on how much you believe in yourself.

4. **How do I stop?** Method itself won't see you through without effort on your part. You must choose the way that best suits your circumstances.

These four key questions are so crucial to your success that we need to look at each one in turn.

14. Why Should I Stop?

At first glance the answer seems obvious. 'Health,' say the experts. But before you accept this as your own reason, think about your attitude to your health. How much do you value it? Has smoking already affected it? How much discomfort are you prepared to tolerate? For example, do you consider your 'smoker's cough' to be a normal part of your daily life, or does that increasing tightness in your chest worry you a little? The importance you attach to the effects of smoking on health does not depend on the lurid details I can give you about smoking, but on *how much you perceive yourself to be at risk*.

How Can Smoking Affect Me?

Try doing the following 'Smoker's Awareness Quiz'. It will help you focus on what is at stake for you. Can you answer the following ten questions on smoking? Check your answers with the answers on pages 86–89 (more than one answer may be correct in each question).

1. Which of the following is responsible for the largest number of deaths per year in Britain?
   (a) Road accidents
   (b) Cigarette smoking
   (c) Suicides

2. Roughly what proportion of smokers are likely to die as a result of their habit?
   (a) 1 in 1,000
   (b) 1 in 300
   (c) 1 in 3

3. Which of the following statements are true?
   (a) It is safe to smoke ten cigarettes a day.
   (b) Those who smoke cigarettes with a low tar/nicotine yield have a reduced risk of developing lung cancer compared with high tar/nicotine smokers.
   (c) It is less harmful to smoke two packs of low tar/nicotine cigarettes a day than one pack of high tar/nicotine.
   (d) It is safe to smoke cigars.

4. What are the chances of a heavy cigarette smoker (25+ cigarettes a day) developing lung cancer?
   (a) 1 in 5,000
   (b) 1 in 100
   (c) 1 in 4

5. Which of the following is currently the most important cause of chronic bronchitis?
   (a) Industrial air pollution, e.g. coal dust
   (b) Cigarette smoking
   (c) Car exhaust fumes

6. Which of the following are known causes of lung cancer?
   (a) Car exhaust fumes
   (b) General air pollution
   (c) Occupational exposure to asbestos
   (d) Cigarette smoking

7. A person who has had a heart attack, and stops smoking:
   (a) Halves the risk of another attack
   (b) Has the same risk of having another attack
   (c) Reduces the risk of a further attack to that of a non-smoker.

8. Cigarette smoking increases the risk of which of the following:
   (a) Breast cancer
   (b) An earlier menopause
   (c) Influenza
   (d) TB
   (e) Duodenal ulcers

9. Women who both take the contraceptive pill and smoke increase their risk of developing which of the following conditions:
   (a) Cancer of the ovary
   (b) Cancer of the cervix
   (c) Heart attack
   (d) Stroke

10. The following is a list of possible harmful effects that smoking in pregnancy can have on the baby. Which four has smoking been *proven* to increase?
    (a) Having a premature baby
    (b) Miscarriage
    (c) Congenital abnormalities and deformities
    (d) Retarded intellectual function in the baby
    (e) A reduced birthweight
    (f) A reduction in the subsequent height of the child

Answers[1-3]

Add up your marks for correct answers as follows:

1. (a) −2 (b) +5 (c) −2

Smoking causes roughly *seven* times as many premature deaths in the UK each year as road accidents.

2. (a) −2   (b) −2   (c)+5

Overall, very few smokers get off scot-free. In a lifetime's smoking 20 cigarettes a day you will inhale at least 100lb of tar and nicotine.

3. (a) −2   (b) +5   (c) −2   (d) −2

(a) The only safe cigarette is an unlit one! No matter how moderately you think you smoke, your risk of ill-health is always higher than a non-smoker's. Researchers have shown that smokers die, on average, 10–15 years before their time.[4]

(b) The more tar and nicotine your cigarettes yield (see Tables on pages 112–113), the greater your risk of lung cancer and heart disease.

Those who smoke low tar/nicotine cigarettes reduce their risk of these diseases by about a quarter compared with high tar/nicotine smokers. *This only holds true if you do not inhale more, puff more often, or increase the number of cigarettes you smoke.* That is why (c) is the wrong answer: your risk of ill-health is actually *increased* if you double the number of low tar cigarettes you smoke. Low tar cigarettes are no passport to protection.

(d) Cigars carry the same (or even higher) risk of ill-health as cigarettes if you inhale the smoke. Cigars are less hazardous *only if you do not inhale*.

4. (a) −2   (b) −2   (c) +5

One in five people who smoke 25 or more cigarettes a day will develop lung cancer. Those smoking 15–25 a day have a risk of 1 in 8.

5. (a) 0   (b) 5   (c) −2

There is no good evidence that car fumes have any measurable effect on the incidence of chronic bronchitis or emphysema, another disabling chest disease which develops alongside bronchitis, and causes progressive destruction of lung tissue. Although air that is heavily polluted by smoke from coal does contribute to an increased incidence of chronic bronchitis, (a) is incorrect because smoking is, *by far*, the most important cause. Even coal miners with a high exposure to coal dust owe most of their high rate of chronic bronchitis to cigarettes.

6. (a) −2   (b) −2   (c) +5   (d) +5

(a), (b) & (d). Although city dwellers have higher rates of lung cancer than those living in the countryside, this is largely because they are more likely to smoke. Air pollution and car exhaust fumes contribute little to lung cancer, compared with the enormous effect of cigarettes.

(c) Those who work in the asbestos industry have a higher risk of developing lung cancer. If they smoke cigarettes as well, their risk of lung cancer can be 100 times as great as a non-exposed non-smoker.

7. (a) +5   (b) −2   (c) −2

Smoking is, undoubtedly, a major cause of heart disease, although there are other causes (see Personal Risk Profile, pages 90–92). A heart attack occurs when part of the essential blood supply to the heart is cut off. This prevents oxygen from reaching that portion of the heart muscle which, consequently, dies. The bigger the dead portion of heart muscle, the more serious and life-threatening the heart attack.

(c) is incorrect because a heart attack *always* causes some permanent scarring of the heart muscle. Cigarette smoking probably exerts its effects on the heart through carbon monoxide and/or nicotine by causing the walls of the coronary arteries— carrying the 'lifeblood' of the heart itself—to thicken to such an extent that blood can no longer pass through.

(a) is thus the only correct answer because giving up smoking, while not fully reversing the damage already done, can halve the chances of a further attack. Of all the advice heart attack victims are given, stopping smoking is the only measure that is so far of *proven* value.

8. (a) −2   (b) +5   (c) −2   (d) −2   (e) +5

As far as we know from research, cigarette smoking is not, in any way, associated with breast cancer. (c) and (d) are incorrect because they are diseases caused by a virus and bacterium respectively.

(b) Research has shown that the more you smoke the earlier you are likely to have your menopause. Whereas only about half of non-smoking women aged 44–53 have had their menopause, two-thirds of women who smoke 20 a day have had their menopause. This may be because some of the components of tobacco reduce levels of the female hormone, oestrogen.

(e) Eight or nine in every ten people with duodenal or gastric ulcers smoke cigarettes. Smokers are about twice as likely as non-smokers to develop ulcers. Smoking also delays the healing of such ulcers. Research shows that in non-smokers 70 per cent of ulcers healed within four weeks without any other treatment compared with only 30 per cent in smokers. This seems to be because ulcers thrive in an over-acid environment and smoking may prevent the secretion of adequate amounts of digestive juices, which are essential for neutralising the acid produced in the stomach, and thus encourage the development of an ulcer.

9. (a) −2   (b) −2   (c) +5   (d) +5

(a) and (b) are incorrect as there is no good evidence implicating the Pill or smoking in either of these conditions.

(c) Both the Pill and smoking independently increase the risk of having a heart attack.[5,6] Women who take the Pill are four times more likely, and women who smoke 25+ cigarettes a day are seven times more likely to have a heart attack than non-Pill takers or non-smokers. Taking the Pill *and* smoking compounds the risk of a heart attack to 40 times that of a non-smoking, non-Pill-user. According to recent research, the Pill (and therefore smoking as well) is a more frequent cause of death from heart disease and strokes in young women than all the complications of pregnancy and childbirth combined.[7]

(d) Smoking and the Pill both increase the risk of subarachnoid haemorrhage which is a stroke or haemorrhage beneath the linings of the brain. This can either be fatal, or cause severe disability and difficulty in moving about. The risk of developing such a haemorrhage is multiplied *22-fold* in smokers who take the Pill compared with non-smoking, non-Pill takers.

10. (a) +5   (b) +5   (c) +5   (d) 0   (e) +5   (f) 0

With the exception of (d) and (f) pregnant women who smoke have a small, but significantly increased risk of all the other complications listed. Some researchers have suggested that smoking in pregnancy may have long-term effects on the baby's subsequent intelligence and development, but the evidence is still too tenuous to take seriously. (The research suggesting smoking affects a child's growth showed that children born to heavier smokers were, on average, 1cm shorter than those born to non-smokers; at age 16, this difference disappears altogether.)[8]

How to Assess Your Score

70–80 points: You have a high awareness rating, and fully recognise the dangers of the cigarette.

50–70 points: You have a fair awareness rating, but there is still room for improvement.

0–50 points: You have a poor smoker's awareness. Re-read the answers to the quiz and Chapter 2.

An overall minus score: You really have no appreciation of the effects of smoking. Re-read Chapter 2 and the answers to the quiz very slowly and carefully!

Your Personal Risk Profile

Now that you are fully aware of the risks that the smoker faces—and the female smoker in particular—you can move on to assess your own personal risk. You may escape serious illness, but few smokers escape completely unaffected. Answer YES or NO to each of the following questions, and then score your Risk Profile at the end.

	Yes	No
1. Do you smoke cigarettes (as opposed to other forms of tobacco)?	✓	
2. Did you start smoking at the age of 14 or earlier?		✓
3. Have you smoked for 20 years or more?		✓
4. Do you smoke 15 or more cigarettes a day?	✓	
5. Do you inhale when you smoke?	✓	
6. Do you smoke, or have you spent most of your 'smoking career' smoking cigarettes which yield 20mg or more tar per cigarette (check the tar yield of your brand with the table on pages 112–113)?		✓
7. Are you 35 or over?		✓
8. Does your job involve regular contact with any of the following substances:		
(a) asbestos		
(b) lead		
(c) cadmium		
(d) copper		

	Yes	No
9. Do you live in an industrialised area where the air is polluted?		✓
10. Do you tend to wheeze? (Asthma sufferers discount this question).	✓	
11. Do you often feel a bit of phlegm (or infected mucus) sticks at the back of your nose/throat?	✓	
12. Do you have a chronic cough which never completely goes away?		✓
13. Do you cough up phlegm—especially in the mornings during winter?		✓
14. Do you find you get short of breath under any of following circumstances? (Only part (c) applies if you are over 60):		
(a) When climbing two flights of stairs		✓
(b) When hurrying along the street		✓
(c) When getting dressed		✓
15. Do you eat a lot of animal fat (e.g. butter, red meat, milk, cheese) and fatty foods?	✓	✓
16. Do you have high blood pressure?	✓	
17. Are you taking the contraceptive Pill?		✓
18. Are you diabetic, or does diabetes run in your family?		✓
19. Have any of your parents, sisters or brothers had a heart attack?		✓
20. Would you describe yourself as aggressive, highly strung and competitive?	✓	
21. Have you had your menopause?		✓
22. Do you tend to take very little strenuous exercise?		✓
23. Are you 14lb or more overweight?		✓

	Yes	No
24. Do any members of your family have duo-denal ulcers?		✓
25. Do you have an 'acidic' stomach—i.e. do you tend to get stomach pains when you haven't eaten for a while, which are relieved by food or antacid tablets?	✓	
26. Do you tend to get stomach pains when you feel anxious or upset?		✓

How to Score Your Risk

Score as follows for all the questions to which you have answered YES. The higher your score the bigger the risk.

1–8: *5 points for each*	15: *5 points*
9: *2 points*	16: *5 points*
10: *1 point*	17 & 18: *5 points each*
11: *1 point*	19 & 20: *2 points each*
12: *3 points*	21: *5 points*
13: *5 points*	22 & 23: *1 point each*
14: *4 points for each part*	24 & 25: *2 points each*
	26: *1 point*

Very high risk: 80–100
You could be in serious danger of developing any one of the smoking-induced diseases. Check below to see if you are especially at risk of developing a particular condition. If you are worried, consult your doctor.

High risk: 50–80
You are taking a big chance if you continue smoking.

Medium risk: 20–50
You are still taking a substantial risk.

Low risk: less than 20
Your risk of developing a smoking-induced illness is not high—yet. But it will increase as you continue smoking.

Specific Risk Profile

1. **Your Lung Cancer Risk:**
Add up your scores for questions 1–8. Your total possible score is 40. You have a high risk of developing lung cancer if your score is 35 or more.

2. Your Risk of Chronic Bronchitis:

Add up your scores for questions 1–14. Your total possible score is 64. If you scored 50 or more you have a high risk of developing chronic bronchitis.

3. Your Risk of Heart Disease:

Add up your scores for questions 1–7 and questions 15–23. Your total possible score is 70. You are at high risk of heart disease if your score is 50 or more.

4. Your Risk of Duodenal Ulcer:

Add up your scores for questions 1–7 and 24–26. Your total possible score is 40. If you scored more than 35, your risk of developing a duodenal ulcer is high.

The 'Unofficial' Reasons for Stopping

Health is usually the 'official' reason for giving up smoking, but just as many smokers stop for financial reasons. You may have several kinds of reasons for wanting to stop. In Claudia's case: 'Without a doubt, the most important reason for me was to have control over my body. It was very much a matter of pride to me that I should be able to control what I wanted to do. I found it humiliating and horrible to be dictated to by cigarettes.' Like Claudia, you must gather together as many reasons for stopping as possible. If you are not convinced by your own reasoning you will undoubtedly fail.

15. Will I Get More out of Stopping than Going on Smoking?

Weighing up the Forces

Anti-smoking leaflets and commercials will tell you about the undoubted value of stopping smoking, but they will give you little insight into what *you* get out of cigarettes. Their job, after all, is to persuade you not to smoke. It is your responsibility alone to weigh up the benefits of stopping against those of continuing. What are the special pressures on you to smoke? Every woman will have her personal tug-of-war about it. It is not enough to consider the so-called 'rational' argument alone. Your success depends on the balance you strike between the rational and emotional factors in your life, which together keep you smoking and wanting to stop at the same time. When you have discovered that balance, you will be in a position to change it.

The Benefits of Stopping

Smoking—unlike any other serious health hazard—is a risk with a loophole. If you drunkenly drive into a head-on collision, you can guarantee yourself permanent damage. But even if you smoke for many years, you can actually *reverse* some of the cigarette damage by stopping smoking. If you have smoked for ten years, and then stop, it will take roughly the same amount of time for your risk of lung cancer to return to that of a non-smoker. But you don't have to wait a decade for an improvement in your health. More than nine in every ten smokers with a chronic cough find it completely disappears, or substantially improves in less than a month. And in as many as one-third it vanishes within a fortnight.

Similarly, about three-quarters of smokers who are short of breath notice an improvement very soon after giving up.[1] Thus while lung cancer and heart disease are the ultimate threats over smokers, people are often more acutely aware of the tell-tale early signs of ill-health, which disappear almost magically on giving up.

Although Tanya only managed to stay off cigarettes for two weeks, she immediately noticed a difference in her health: 'I felt miles better. I could breathe more easily within a couple of days. That's probably why I felt a lot more energetic. I felt, for the first time, that air was really getting down into my lungs when I breathed. Before I stopped, the air would go *down*, but none would go *in*. It was lovely to be able to lie back in bed and breathe properly—I could never breathe lying down before I stopped, I was too chesty.'

Barbara, who stopped six years ago, admits the main thing she noticed when she first stopped was a marvellous sense of superiority over the poor sods who were still addicted . . . I don't know whether I was *actually* healthier, but I certainly felt great. I hadn't smoked long enough for cigarettes to visibly impair my health, but it felt so good to know that you could go anywhere at any time of day or night, without worrying where the nearest cigarette machine was. It felt like a release from a self-inflicted imprisonment.'

What Do You Get Out of Smoking?

Having a good reason for stopping is not enough. You need to examine why you can't stop *in spite of* the many good reason you may have for doing so. Is it something to do with the 'stress' in your life? Perhaps you smoke when you feel bored or insecure. But *why* is your life so stressful or boring? Why do you feel insecure and reach for your cigarettes when perhaps your husband, male friends or colleagues at work stopped years ago?

Understanding Your Need To Smoke

To understand this, you must take over where the research leaves off. There is a big difference between the way the researcher sees you as a *smoker*, and the way you see yourself as a person who happens to smoke. The researcher tries to understand your problem by isolating you and your smoking from your surroundings. Only you can place yourself back in the *real* world in order to see what kind of priority smoking has in your life. Because smoking is always a complex habit, I suggest that the best way to understand your own reasons for smoking is to look at the problem from three different perspectives:

1. Your smoking career
2. Your cues for smoking
3. Your feelings and your need for cigarettes

Your Smoking Career

Go back to the beginning. Try to remember your very first cigarette—who gave it to you and under what sort of circumstances. Most of all, try to think back to why you wanted that cigarette. Did you feel forced? What were you trying to prove? Or was it just curiosity?

Pursue your smoking career step by step, and try to connect up important phases in your life with changes in your smoking. When did you become a regular smoker? When did cigarettes become an indispensable part of your life? Did leaving school, getting a new job or moving to a new place have any influence on your smoking? Were you ever aware of smoking a specific brand in order to create a particular impression? Who were you trying to impress? Think back, too, to the people who have been important in your life, starting with your parents. Can you single out any female or male friends who had any special influences on your smoking patterns? Try to match the amount you smoked with changing phases in your life, and you might surprise yourself with the picture you uncover. If there are any great fluctuations in the amount you smoke each day, what are the circumstances which lead you to smoke heavily? Do you smoke more just before a period, for example?

Tanya's smoking career began when she was 12. She smoked to impress her stepsister. 'I smoked to prove to her that I could do it.' Having left school at 14, Tanya's first job was at a Hatton Garden jewellers. She began smoking regularly then—about ten a day. She didn't really enjoy smoking, but it was the first time she had the money to buy them. It felt adult to smoke and she smoked the same brand as her stepmother. By the time she was 18 she was smoking 20 a day. Smoking was slowly becoming an indispensable part of her life and when her brother challenged her to stop, she surprised herself by losing the bet. 'I never thought any more about it, and just carried on smoking,' says Tanya. Tanya married at 23, and gradually built up the number she smoked to 40 a day. It was not until after the birth of her first child that she recognised her increasing dependence on cigarettes. She smoked 40 a day throughout her second pregnancy and developed a severe chest infection after the baby was born. She could neither breathe nor lie down, but still she continued to smoke. Her relationship with her husband had, by this time, become very strained. She suspected that he was seeing another woman, and he didn't want to take any responsibility for bringing up their children. By the time her youngest was two, Tanya could no longer escape the obvious connection between her shortness of breath and repeated chest infections and her cigarettes. She suddenly had a vision that she might die, as her own mother had, before her children reached their teens. This finally prompted her to get help in giving up at the local smokers' clinic. She managed, for the first time since she had started smoking, to stay off cigarettes for two whole weeks, by which time the storm which had been brewing with her husband finally exploded. She discovered that he did indeed have a girlfriend, who was pregnant; she threw him out of the house. She immediately turned to her cigarettes again. She is now smoking more than she ever did previously: 'I don't think I was ready to give up,' says Tanya. 'I couldn't have faced life at that time without cigarettes. I think I've bitten off more than I can chew. I don't feel I have the strength to look after two kids on my own any more.'

Claudia's smoking career began when she was 11. She remembers lying in bed feeling ill and bored: 'I saw one of my mother's cigarettes lying around, and I tried half.' She associated smoking with the important, serious things her mother did. After that, she only smoked the occasional cigarette when it was offered at the Youth Club or Girl Guides. Her friends smoked. It was 'very much the thing to do then', says Claudia. She was smoking about 20 a week by the age of 17. She became aware that her own untipped brand wasn't quite smart enough, so she changed 'to a more sophisticated-looking American brand'. The decisive factor which changed her smoking pattern was leaving Yorkshire where she grew up to start a new job in London at the age of 19. Her consumption doubled. She felt nervous and insecure in the lonely adult world away from her family and 'cigarettes became a friend.' As time went on she increased from 20 to 30 a day and, by the time she was in her late 20s, she began to view her smoking as a problem. At 28 she ended a very unhappy relationship with a man, after which her cigarette consumption soared to 60 a day. Cigarettes became her immediate response to every sign of distress and the amount she smoked fluctuated daily. She smoked heavily when she felt bad, and was able to cut down when she felt more confident. It was not until nearly ten years later that she felt sufficiently strong to stop. Her need to control her smoking had, by then, overwhelmed her need to continue smoking. She stopped at the age of 37.

Cues for Smoking

To describe smoking as 'just a habit' is a truism—and an unhelpful one at that. It is more important for you to distinguish between those parts of the 'habit' which relate to emotional aspects of your life, and those which do not. Your strategy for dealing with each will be different. The emotionally less important cigarettes are triggered by 'cigarette cues'—the many circumstances under which you find yourself automatically smoking. Don't underestimate the strength of these cues—they are an integral part of your habit. If you can change them, you can cut out the cigarettes which accompany them.

I suggest that the best way to rediscover your cigarette cues—which are often so well ingrained they are hard to recognise

—is to try to stay off cigarettes for a whole day (or a morning if you can't manage a day). Then go slowly through the situations in which you almost always smoke. The following examples of cigarette cues should help you identify your own and you will probably be surprised at how much of your habit really is just habit.

The Early Morning Consciousness Cigarette: Is the first glimmer of light in your dreamworld a cigarette cue? As you automatically reach out to stop the alarm clock, do you also reach out for a cigarette?

The Breakfast Cigarette: Is grasping that first cup of coffee, or picking up the newspaper another cigarette signal?

The Commuter's Cigarette: Have you been sitting in the smoking compartment of the train or bus for years? If you travel everywhere by car, do you automatically reach for a cigarette the moment you get your car going?

The Telephone Cigarette: Do you have an automatic reflex in which you reach for the receiver with one hand, and a cigarette with the other.

The 'Me Too' Cigarette: Do you always smoke when others offer or in situations when others are smoking? This response may be emotional in part, but it is also very much an automatic reflex.

The Mid-Morning Break Cigarette: Is your break somehow incomplete without a cigarette?

The 'Smoking Is Permitted' Cigarette: Do you always find yourself smoking in restaurants and cinemas where smoking is permitted just because it *is* permitted?

The Concentration Cigarette: Do you always smoke when you have to concentrate?

The 'What shall I do with my free hand' Cigarette: Do you find that under some circumstances, especially when you are sitting still in one place 'trapped' into inaction, you always smoke?

There are many other cigarette cues to which you are so accustomed that they have become subconscious—the TV cigarette, the after-dinner cigarette, and the ubiquitous drink cigarette, the after-sex cigarette and the night-cap cigarette.

Feelings and Cigarette Need

Your cigarette need forms the missing link between your smoking career and your cigarette cues. It is the emotional cement upon which your habit is founded and it is one of the outward signs of the stresses you experience as a woman. It may be a specific response—because you are angry with your boss, irritated by your children, humiliated by your lover. On the other hand, it may be part of a more general response to the long-term stresses in your life—the isolation of long periods at home with the children for instance. Or you feel you're too fat. Because you're angry with your lot, but can't express it in any other way? (see Chapter 5) In many cases, your cigarette need will be bound up with your cigarette cues, but you should be able to trace your smoking back to your feelings as well as to your cigarette cues.

Smoking for Mrs D. is a release from what she describes as the 'unendurable tensions' of being married to a schizophrenic. Her smoking patterns reflect both responses to immediate crises in her life, as well as the continuing stress of her marital responsibilities. On the one hand, says Mrs D.: 'My husband's aggro sends me rushing to buy cigarettes.' But she also recognises her underlying reasons for needing cigarettes too: 'I think that I smoke from boredom and despair, as there is no foreseeable end to my marriage predicament. I might as well go one way as the other. I know the risks which, in my case, are aggravated by a tendency to bronchial troubles, but choose to ignore them.'

Lorraine describes herself as a 'compulsive smoker, eater, sipper and nail-biter.' She was fat as a child and is constantly waging a battle against weight gain. She has always postponed any serious attempts to stop smoking because she feels she may gain even more weight: 'I've been told that I will put on even more weight if I stop. That, to me, is like saying that a ten-ton lorry load will drop on your head tomorrow. I'm not prepared to run the risk of gaining even more weight.' Lorraine has high blood pressure and had to stop taking the Pill but, 'It is more disfiguring to gain weight,' she says, 'than to risk the consequences of continuing to smoke.'

16. Have I the Confidence to Stop?

Ex-smokers—as we have already seen—are achievers. Have you reached the stage in your life when you feel sufficiently confident in yourself and your ability to succeed?

After numerous unsuccessful attempts to stop, Clara began to regard giving up as something that only others could achieve and each time she failed she felt less and less confident. Stopping became a crucial test of her self-esteem: 'I used to think that if I could stop smoking I could do anything. But smoking meant too much to me then. I didn't yet have the confidence or the emotional equipment to get through the panics without cigarettes.' When she finally did stop for good, she says her reasons for success were 'not specifically connected with my smoking at all, but rather with the changing relationship I had with myself and the world. It was one which slowly enabled me to believe in myself a bit more. Giving up was part of starting afresh, and leaving the old lack of confidence behind.'

The Big When?

Like Clara, you won't succeed till you're ready. And that readiness to stop, although it depends in part on your view of the health risks you are taking, also depends on your state of mind. If you are feeling miserable and battered, it is hardly worth aggravating your mood with repeated unsuccessful attempts to stop. The courage in giving up lies not so much in the act itself, but in how you perceive your personal power, and only you can decide when the time is right.

The Confidence Test[1]

How self-confident a person are you? Have you ever dared to sit down and assess yourself truthfully? This test should give you a rough guide to how you feel about yourself in general and about your ability to stop smoking in particular. Don't be dishonest—there is only one person you can cheat!

How to Test Your Self-Confidence Rating

Tick the box which most closely resembles how you feel about each of the following statements. Try to avoid the 'uncertain' box if you can:

	strongly agree	mildly agree	uncertain	mildly disagree	strongly disagree
1. I am satisfied with myself on the whole					
2. I feel that I have a number of good qualities					
3. I feel that I do not have much to be proud of					
4. I am able to do things as well as most people					
5. I wish I could have more respect for myself					
6. All in all, I am inclined to feel that I am a failure					
7. I believe that I shall be able to stop smoking for good					
8. Even if the circumstances were right, I would find it hard to stop smoking					
9. It would be relatively easy for me to cut down the number I smoke by half					
10. I know that I shall be successful in stopping smoking when the time is right					

How to Score

Questions 1, 2, 4, 7, 9, 10:
Score 10 points if you **strongly agree**
     5 points if you **mildly agree**
     2 points if you are **uncertain**
     1 points if you **mildly disagree**
     0 points if you **strongly disagree**
Questions 3, 5, 6, 8:
Score 10 points if you **strongly disagree**
     5 points if you **mildly disagree**
     2 points if you are **uncertain**
     1 point if you **mildly agree**
     0 points if you **strongly agree**

Your General Self-Confidence Rating

Add up your scores for *ALL* the questions. You could have scored a maximum of 100 points.
High self-confidence: 70+ points
Fair self-confidence: 40–70 points
Low self-confidence: Under 40

Your Ability to Stop Smoking

Add up your scores for questions 7–10. You could have scored a maximum of 40 points.

If you scored 30+: you have a strong belief in your ability to stop smoking. It therefore follows that your chances of success are equally high.
If you scored 20–30: you are not quite as sure as you might be of your ability to stop smoking. But with a little encouragement you could acquire the confidence that will lead to success.
If you scored less than 20: you haven't got much confidence in your ability to stop smoking *at the moment*. You will need a great deal of encouragement and support if you are ever to stop for good.

17. How Do I Stop?

The Deciding Factor

Assuming that you have found one or several good reasons to give up, and have convinced yourself that the benefits outweigh those of smoking—it is your Self-Confidence Rating (see Chapter 16) that will decide how you go about giving up. A HIGH Self-Confidence Rating means you will probably be able to go it alone with the minimum of difficulty. But a FAIR or, especially, a LOW score on the Self-Confidence Test means that you need some help in your efforts to stop and that you will probably benefit from group support. Of course the *kind* of support you choose is entirely up to you. If you prefer a formal group, there is a list of organisations at the end of the book (Appendix I) which will put you in touch with your nearest smokers' group. In my experience however, you will, by now, have reached the stage when you do not really need formal or 'expert' help. In this case the best form of support for you could come from a self-help group.

The Value of the Self-Help Group

There is a good reason to believe that the group approach has special value for women. First, research in the early 1970s shows quite clearly that, while male success rates in giving up smoking are not affected by whether or not they receive group support, the proportion of women who stop on their own is only half that of men. Ellen Gritz, a research psychologist at the University of California, Los Angeles, confirmed this recently by showing that, in six separate studies in which there was precious little personal contact between therapist and client, the men always had higher success rates for stopping than the women.[1] The way to maximize success for the women, she concluded, is to provide an atmosphere of support for the women concerned. Most women who have participated in all-female self-help groups recognise only too well that they derive support from the group *because it is all-female*; scientists have all but ignored this in their research. Some supporting evidence came to light only by accident when Canadian researchers working at a smokers' clinic in Toronto found, to their surprise, that the usual success rate for women was 20 per cent (compared with nearly 40 per cent in men), but rose to 30 per cent when the group was all-female.[2]

Claudia attended a group for two months. She not only got support, but even self-satisfaction from it: 'The group was important. I enjoyed it, and it gave me a good boost. Each week when I felt my spirits beginning to flag, I would go there. I found that talking to peple who were still smoking and having problems reinforced my desire not to smoke. It made me feel very good. I felt a sense of achievement which was hard to get in the office. There was a lot of feedback, and people would tell me how good I was for staying off cigarettes. It mattered that they were taking the whole thing very seriously.'

There is sense in smokers seeking out other smokers, rather than expert non-smokers, to share their difficulties and progress. Talking about giving up smoking is a bit like trying to describe a very familiar pain that has finally resolved itself. When it is there, it is vivid and uppermost in your mind and, when it is gone, it seems a vague indistinct memory. That is why ex-smokers will frustrate you with their woolly nonchalance while non-smokers may find it incomprehensible that you should allow yourself to fall victim to such a 'disgusting' habit in the first place. Within a group you will find that everyone has a vested interest in your progress. No one will get bored and the support you derive from it will help you prepare for giving up.

If you feel you would rather give up on your own or with a friend, there is no reason why you shouldn't adapt my suggestions on group work and methods. Remember my outline is for you to adopt, modify or reject.

How to Find a Group

If you already belong to a women's group or local women's health organisation, then you have a ready-made group. Find out from other group members if there are other women who would seriously like to stop smoking. It's best to keep groups small with no more than six to eight people. If you are not a member of any particular group, but would like to start one, you could try the idea out with some friends, colleagues at work or neighbours. If you feel daunted by the idea of setting up a group on your own, then contact your nearest smoking-and-health agency (see Appendix I for advice).

Meetings

It is important to meet regularly, and to keep in close touch with one another. Meet somewhere comfortable and private where you can talk freely. It is a good idea to stick to a non-smoking rule at meetings. The number of times you meet will vary according to the needs of individual members and you may well want to meet more than once a week initially. Once you agree to meet, stick to the arrangement. Group members can keep in close touch by phone or visits between meetings when support can be crucial. An emergency phone call in a moment of temptation may see you or someone else through.

Using the Group

The great thing about using a self-help group is that there are no rights and wrongs. Whatever feels right *is* right. If you feel a bit unsure about how to get started, don't worry: you'll get better with practice.

1. Start by answering the four key questions (see Chapter 13). It is important to get these right. Take as much time as you need, and make sure that *everyone* has enough time to discuss their answers as fully as possible. It may help to go away and think about it, or even write down what your cigarette cues and needs are, and then bring your answers back to the group.

2. Inform yourself as fully as you can about the health issues raised by smoking. Make sure you are fully aware of how smoking affects your own personal health—the quizzes on pages 85 and 90 should help. If you want any further information, the smoking-and-health organisations listed in Appendix I will be glad to help.

3. How do you feel about cigarette advertising? Do you feel exploited by the tobacco companies? What are you going to do about it?

4. Agreeing on a date for stopping is essential. You must make sure all members are happy about the date and are prepared to stick to it. There is little point in collectively throwing your cigarettes away in a dramatic gesture at the very first meeting if you are not yet ready to see it through.

5. The method you use to give up is not of central importance.

Anything goes, from carrot-chewing to using mechanical filters. You may want to try one method as a group, but giving up is a very personal matter and it may be easier for each of you to use whichever method suits you best—any of the six I suggest below or one of your own making. Whichever you choose, it is important to discuss with the group how you plan to face up to giving up.
6. Don't forget that stopping smoking does not immediately make you into an ex-smoker. Don't assume you won't need any more support from the group the minute you stop. The period when you hover between being a smoker and an ex-smoker is dangerous; you may find you need more support at this stage than at any other time. And even if you find you can manage by yourself with the minimum of effort, you may find you can help others gain strength from your own success.

Six Ideas

There is no reason why you shouldn't use parts of each of these methods or combine several. The final decision on strategy rests with you. Use these suggestions as *a guide* only.

1. *Stopping 'Cold'*

This means deciding when to stop, and then doing it. It sounds too easy, but is the commonest (and most successful) method used. Coming to your decision is, therefore, the most important part of this method. If you are a fastidious sort of person you can set yourself a date in advance, and do a count down to 'D-Day'. Choose a special day, such as a pay rise or your birthday. Try to choose a time when you are likely to be under minimum stress. Alternatively, you could stop the moment you get a cold or cough—but don't use this as a method of evasion. Don't be deterred if you have tried this way before—and failed: it was probably because you were not really ready to face life without cigarettes.

2. *Smoke Yourself Sick*

Decide when you are going to stop, and then smoke double the number of cigarettes you normally smoke two days beforehand. On the day beforehand, smoke three (or even four) times as many cigarettes. The principle of this method, of course, is to disgust yourself and to smoke yourself to the point at which you find cigarettes revoltingly unpleasant. This should give you added

willpower to stay off cigarettes when D-Day arrives. Smoke every last cigarette you can find. If you are used to smoking mild cigarettes, then smoke different, strong-tasting cigarettes in the two days before stopping. And don't forget that doubling the amount you smoke also means puffing twice as much as well. Chain smoke on the last day and on the evening before D-Day, find yourself a couple of quiet hours—probably before you go to bed. All you need is your remaining cigarettes (keep five), a lighter, and a watch. Light the first cigarette, and, keeping an eye on the watch take a puff and inhale deeply every six seconds. Carry on doing this until you feel sick, or can't take it any more. Give yourself no more than a few minutes' break, and then start again. Continue the six-second puffing process until you have got through your five remaining cigarettes, or until you feel you really never want a cigarette again. Go to bed immediately, don't hang around contemplating your fate. Your ex-smoker's career awaits you.
CAUTION: DO NOT USE THIS METHOD if you already have chest or heart disease—it could be dangerous.

3. *The Miserly Approach*

This method is also based on simple, but sound principles. Work out how much you spend on cigarettes each day. If you are attempting to stop as a group, set up a communal 'fund' into which you all place the amount you spend per day on cigarettes. If there are six of you in the group, all smoking two packs per day, then you will collectively accumulate more than £200 in only six weeks. If you really mean business, why not open an ex-smokers' bank account and make someone in the group responsible for paying your collective cigarette money into the account? When money has accumulated over, say, an eight-week period, celebrate with some of the proceeds. There are, of course, many varia-tions on this theme. You could get those who lapse back to the odd cigarette to pay a forfeit—say, 50 pence—into the fund, but do make sure that everyone fully agrees to being penalised since it may serve to depress rather than encourage those who waver.

4. *Temporary, Permanent Stopping*

If the idea of giving up for ever still seems a daunting prospect to you, then set yourself a short-term target first. Your first task is to prove to yourself that you can stay off cigarettes for a specified time, *because you have decided to do so*. Try to think of it as a dress-rehearsal for the real thing. The length of the 'test period' depends entirely on how difficult you perceive giving up smoking to be. For instance, if you have never been able to go without a cigarette for more than a day then try for two days first. When you have reached the first milestone successfully, you should feel more confident about setting the next—lengthening the test period each time. This way may seem more painless than method No. 1, but in fact it is not very different, except that the decision you take seems less awesome than stopping cold.

Many smokers go through this process unconsciously—they attempt to stop, go back to cigarettes, and then regard themselves as failures. Don't be discouraged—nearly all ex-smokers have a series of 'false starts' before they stop successfully. The potential ex-smoker is only a failure *until she is a success*.

This method allows you to build up your confidence by *planning* your practice runs rather than feeling miserable each time you seem to 'relapse'. Each 'relapse' becomes a step towards your ultimate success.

5. *Estranged Smoking*

This is a good method for very exacting people. It involves reversing the smoking cues, and requires patient adherence. Set a date for stopping, perhaps one to four weeks ahead, and confound your habit little by little. Start by smoking a different brand of cigarettes, preferably one you don't like. Change the brand again as soon as you become accustomed to it. Smoke with the opposite hand. Hold the cigarette between your second and third fingers. Use matches if you normally use a lighter. Try to avoid the usual cigarette cues, and smoke at unusual times instead. Why not ban smoking everywhere at home except in the loo, or when sitting in a certain chair? If you find it hard to handle all the cues at once, then concentrate on avoiding them one by one.

This method can be fun, and should give you an insight into why you smoke. Discuss what you learn about your habit with the rest of the group. This is an especially good method for distinguishing the 'habit' from the 'need' for cigarettes. Once you have actually stopped, you may need considerable support in the initial stages: although you will have learned, in the early stages, to deal effectively with your cigarette cues you will still have to face your cigarette need (see pages 95–99).

6. *Gradual Stopping*

This method sounds the easiest, but is often the most taxing and is much like running a guerilla offensive against yourself. Each day you must cut down smoking a little, and each day will therefore confront you with many new decisions about smoking. Nevertheless, if you stick to your regime, the gradual approach does have its merits. You can reduce your health risk whether you stop completely or just end up smoking less.

This method should appeal to the planners and organisers. It is important to devise a timetable for cutting down. It should be reasonably strict, but flexible enough to alter if you find it tough going. Try to think of it as a fitness programme that operates in stages. Don't progress from one stage to the next until you feel you are ready to handle it. If you feel yourself slipping back, don't give up entirely, just go back a stage or so and build up again. The time you spend on each stage is, again, entirely up to you, but collective pressure from your group to reduce to nil by a certain date—four to eight weeks for example—may give you the extra impetus you need to stick to your schedule. There are two important points about your schedule. If your objective is to stop, then you must plan not just cutting down, but cutting down to *nil*. Second, don't set yourself impossible tasks. The underlying principle of this method is gradual reduction—no more than 20 per cent each week. So if you smoke a pack a day, and decide to stop over a five-week period, cut down to 16 a day for the first week, and 12 for the second, and so forth. If you find it impossible to stick to the 12 a day regime, you can always return temporarily to 16 a week. It does not matter if your final nil-date is shifted back a little—what matters is that you reach it successfully.

There are, of course, other ways of gradually cutting down your smoking. You could make it easier for yourself, for example, by alternating cutting down the number of cigarettes you smoke with a week of smoking the *same* number of cigarettes, but a lower tar brand. Or you could use one of the commercially available filters to further reduce your intake of toxic substance (see page 114).

If you really Can't Stop

I believe there is a small group of smokers who will never be able to stop. But there are no easy ways of knowing whether you are likely to fall into this group. You are your own best judge of this. Learn to trust your own feelings about your need to smoke. You may know only too well that the time is not yet right for you. But remember not to judge how entrenched your smoking is by your previous attempts to stop. There are two questions you must answer before you can decide whether you really can't stop:

1. *Have I tried?* Don't settle for anything less than success until you have convinced yourself you really have tried. It is important to examine why you haven't been able to stop. Perhaps the group can help you adopt a more successful future strategy. It may seem obvious, but no-one should accept that they can't stop *until they have tried*—at least once in earnest. There is little difference between the smoker who insists it's impossible to stop and the non-smoker who insists that people smoke because they are stupid or ignorant.

2. *Have I tried hard enough?* You only have your judgement to follow here. If you can convince everyone else in the group that you really can't stop, perhaps you are justified in rethinking your smoking problem. Don't fall into the trap of using previous half-baked attempts at giving up to justify never trying again. But whatever you decide, don't settle for failure. If you don't stop completely, there is other action that you can take. So far as your health is concerned, there is no alternative that is as good as giving up, but you can successfully reduce the risk you take even if you continue smoking. If you choose this option, try to think of it as a step towards success in the future.

The Strategy for Reducing Your Risk

This depends on paying close attention to two things:
    What you smoke
    The way you smoke

What You Smoke

Here are a few simple rules:

1. Make sure you always smoke a filter-tipped brand. You might like to try switching to a brand that contains dark, air-cured tobacco rather than the usual light, Virginia tobacco (see pages 112-113). (It is more difficult to inhale dark tobacco.)

2. The most important way of reducing your risk is to make sure that you smoke a brand that produces as little tar and nicotine as you can accept *without* increasing the number you smoke. Try to

110

opt for brands which produce less than 5 mg tar per cigarette (see pages 112–113). Watch out that you don't compensate for the lower tar levels either by inhaling more deeply or puffing more frequently. Although it is important to reduce both the tar and nicotine intake, you only really need pay attention to the tar yields of the brand you choose, because a low tar cigarette is automatically low in nicotine too.

3. Researchers believe that the carbon monoxide you inhale in cigarette smoke is implicated in heart disease. Minimising your carbon monoxide intake is not such an easy matter because a cigarette with a low tar yield does not ncessarily mean that the carbon monoxide yield is also low. The guide to cigarettes low in carbon monoxide (pages 112–113) should help.

The Way You Smoke

Again, there are a few simple rules to follow:

1. Try to inhale as little as possible, although this is easier said than done.

2. Try to take fewer puffs of each cigarette, and make each one short so that you have as little time as possible to inhale.

3. Never smoke the last third of the cigarette—it is the most dangerous part where the tar and toxic materials in the smoke become concentrated. If you are likely to forget, then mark each cigarette beforehand when you open a new pack.

4. Never re-light a half-smoked cigarette—however much it offends your sense of waste. When a cigarette goes out, some of the harmful tar condenses and concentrates at the burnt end, and you inhale this when you re-light it.

5. Never leave a cigarette in your mouth between puffs. This will minimise the amount you inhale.

Tar & Nicotine Yields of Cigarettes

As determined by the Government Chemist from samples obtained during the period April to September 1979

These brands have a low carbon monoxide yield

†*These brands contain dark, air-cured tobacco*

	Tar yield mg/cig	Nicotine yield mg/cig
Low Tar		
Embassy Ultra Mild	Under 4	under 0.3
John Player King Size Ultra Mild	Under 4	under 0.3
Silk Cut Ultra Mild with Substitute	Under 4	under 0.3
Silk Cut King Size with Substitute	7	0.8
Consulate Menthol	8	0.6
Dunhill International Superior Mild	8	0.7
Embassy Premier King Size	8	0.5
Peter Stuyvesant Extra Mild King Size	8	0.7
Piccadilly Mild	8	0.5
Consulate No. 2	9	0.5
Dunhill King Size Superior Mild	9	0.7
*Embassy Extra Mild	9	0.8
Embassy No. 1 Extra Mild	9	0.7
*John Player King Size Extra Mild	9	0.7
John Player King Size with NSM	9	0.8
Peer Special Extra Mild King Size (with Cytrel)	9	0.7
Player's No. 6 Extra Mild	9	0.7
*Silk Cut	9	0.8
Silk Cut International	9	0.9
*Silk Cut King Size	9	0.9
Silk Cut No. 5	9	0.8
Belair Menthol Kings	10	0.7
Embassy No. 5 Extra Mild	10	0.8
Player's No. 10 with NSM	10	0.7
*Silk Cut No. 3	10	0.8
Low to Middle Tar		
†Gauloises Filter Mild	11	0.5
†Gauloises Longues	11	0.6
St. Moritz	11	0.8
†Gitanes International	12	1.0
John Player Carlton Premium	12	1.2
Player's No. 10 Extra Mild	12	0.8
John Player Carlton King Size	13	1.5
John Player Carlton Long Size	13	1.4
Peer Special Mild King Size (with Cytrel)	13	1.2
†Gauloises Disque Bleu	14	0.7
†Gitanes Caporal Filter	14	0.7
Kensitas Club Mild King Size	14	1.4
Merit	14	1.2
Peter Stuyvesant King Size	14	1.1
Piccadilly No. 7	14	1.0
State Express 555 Medium Mild King Size	14	1.2

Benson & Hedges Sovereign Mild	15	1.3
Black Cat No. 9	15	1.1
Cadets	15	1.2
†Camel Filter Tip	15	1.1
Chesterfield King Size Filter	15	1.2
Craven 'A' Cork Tipped (P)	15	1.2
Dunhill King Size	15	1.3
†Gauloises Caporal Filter	15	0.7
Kensitas Club Mild	15	1.3
Kensitas Mild King Size	15	1.4
Kent	15	1.1
L & M Filter	15	1.2
More Menthol	15	1.5
Pall Mall Filter	15	1.4
Rothmans International	15	1.3
Three Castles Filter	15	1.1
Guards	16	1.1
Kensitas Corsair Mild	16	1.3
Lark Filter Tip	16	1.5
Marlboro	16	1.3
More	16	1.6
Phillip Morris International	16	1.3
Piccadilly Filter De Luxe	16	1.3
Rothmans Royals	16	1.4

Middle Tar

Du Maurier	17	1.5
Dunhill International	17	1.5
Lucky Strike King Size Filter	17	1.4
Piccadilly King Size	17	1.5
Silva Thins	17	1.6
State Express 555 Filter Kings	17	1.4
State Express 555 Selected Virginia (P)	17	1.3
Benson & Hedges Gold Bond	18	1.5
Benson & Hedges Gold Bond King Size	18	1.7
Benson & Hedges King Size	18	1.7
Benson & Hedges Supreme	18	1.8
Embassy Envoy	18	1.4
Embassy Filter	18	1.5
Embassy No. 1 King Size	18	1.4
Embassy No. 3 Standard Size	18	1.5
Embassy Regal	18	1.5
Emperor King Size	18	1.4
Fribourg & Treyer No. 1 Filter De Luxe	18	1.5
Imperial International	18	1.6
John Player King Size	18	1.5
John Player Special	18	1.6
Kensitas Club King Size	18	1.6
Kensitas Tipped King Size	18	1.6

Lambert & Butler International Size	18	1.5
Lambert & Butler King Size	18	1.5
Piccadilly No. 1 (P)	18	1.4
Player's Filter Virginia	18	1.4
Player's Gold Leaf	18	1.5
Player's Medium Navy Cut (P)	18	1.4
Player's No. 6 Filter	18	1.3
Player's No. 6 King Size	18	1.6
Player's No. 6 Plain (P)	18	1.2
Regal King Size	18	1.4
Rothmans King Size	18	1.4
Slim Kings	18	1.4
Sobranie Virginia International	18	1.6
State Express 555 International	18	1.6
Weights Plain (P)	18	1.2
Woodbine Plain (P)	18	1.6
Benson & Hedges Sovereign	19	1.5
Capstan Medium (P)	19	1.4
Embassy Gold	19	1.4
Embassy King Size	19	1.4
Embassy Plain	19	1.4
Gallaher's De Luxe Green (P)	19	1.5
Gold Flake (P)	19	1.4
Kensitas Club	19	1.5
Kensitas Corsair	19	1.4
Kensitas Plain (P)	19	1.6
Nerit	19	1.6
Park Drive Plain (P)	19	1.6
Park Drive Tipped	19	1.5
Player's No. 10	19	1.3
Senior Service Plain (P)	19	1.5
Sterling	19	1.6
Winston King Size	19	1.5
Woodbine Filter	19	1.3

Middle to High Tar

Lucky Strike Plain (P)	24	1.7
Gitanes Caporal Plain (P)	25	1.4
Gallaher's De Luxe Blue (P)	26	2.3
Gauloises Caporal Plain (P)	26	1.3
Capstan Full Strength (P)	28	3.1
Pall Mall King Size (P)	28	2.4

New brands introduced during Apr. 79 to Sep. 79 not yet analysed by the Government Chemist for a period of 6 months.

Silk Cut Extra Mild	6	0.7
Craven A King Size Special Mild	8	0.6
Craven A King Size	17	1.4
Kent De Luxe Length	17	1.3

18. Coping

Are there Any Aids Which Will Help?

If you are looking for a magic pill to stop smoking for you, forget it. You can go out and buy all kinds of anti-smoking remedies. None is a substitute for determination. There are no short cuts to success—you need concentrated effort to stop smoking. Having said that, here are a number of aids which you may find helpful provided you use them to *supplement* your willpower and not to *replace* it. As the pressure on smokers to stop increases, anti-smoking remedies are becoming as potentially profitable as slimming aids. And like slimming aids, they should be treated with a bit of scepticism. Aids can be broadly divided into three main groups: mechanical (the most popular), astringent or 'aversion' therapy and nicotine substitutes.

1. *Mechanical Aids*

There are several kinds of cigarette-holders that reduce the amount of harmful substances such as tar, nicotine and carbon monoxide you inhale. MD4 and its American equivalent, Water Pik, is the most popular. It comprises a set of four re-usable filters which extract progressively larger proportions (25%, 30%, 70% and 90%) of the tar and nicotine out of the smoke you inhale. The theory behind the filters is that the smoker can gradually wean her/himself off cigarettes over an eight-week period, and is then, according to the manufacturers, 'best able to stop smoking altogether'. The 'best' method—and undoubtedly the quickest—is stopping abruptly, but filters do reduce your exposure to the dangerous substances in tobacco smoke.

2. *Aversion Therapy*

The active ingredient in aversion therapy is usually silver nitrate (or potassium permanganate). There are several kinds of tablets, mouthwashes, or sprays available which work by causing an extremely unpleasant taste in the mouth whenever you smoke cigarettes. As long as you don't smoke, they taste mildly minty and the effect supposedly lasts for up to four hours. Their efficacy has never been properly tested. You may find that one of these aids helps; on the other hand you may find you give up the aid instead of the smoking! Products available include Tabmint Chewing Gum, Respaton Tablets, Formula 7 Mouthwash and Nicofin Spray.

3. *Nicotine Substitutes*

The most promising nicotine substitute is a chewing gum ('Nicorette') which contains nicotine. Chewing the gum releases nicotine which can be absorbed into the blood through the membranes lining the mouth. This approach is, of course, based on the assumption that the need for cigarettes is based upon nicotine dependence alone—which is only part of the story (see chapter 4) and that the gum can minimise the craving for cigarettes. Preliminary tests of the gum are mildly encouraging. About 70 per cent of smokers chewing the gum can give up successfully, although after one year the proportion of those still off cigarettes dwindles to about one-third.[1] If you want to try the gum as part of an initial cutting down strategy, you must get it on prescription from your doctor.

Coping without Cigarettes

To be able to cope effectively you will, of course, want to know what to expect when you stop. How hard will it be? Is the so-called 'Smoker's Withdrawal Syndrome' inevitable? What symptoms can you expect, if any, and how long will they last?

For Claudia, the first two days after stopping were the worst: 'I became very physical. I hardly slept at all for the first few nights. I kept jumping up and down, and couldn't sit still. But it was all right because I knew I had made it. I did get some spooky feelings like, what if a cigarette finds its way into my hand? I was scared that I might find one there out of sheer habit. I even dreamt that I was smoking: there was a cigarette and an ashtray, and I picked up the cigarette and smoked it. I was knocked out after the first day and night. But I began to realise that it wasn't so bad. It was quite a revelation to me that I managed to get through all that time without a cigarette—it was terrific. I wasn't going to give way that lightly: after the initial trial there was no longer any reason to give in.'

115

Alison has tried to stop several times in the last two years. But she has not been able to make it: 'After about 12 hours without a cigarette I begin to feel faint. It's rather like the sensation one experiences when going without food for too long. I then experience a not-in-this-world sensation. People's voices seem to recede away from me.' Added to this, Alison says, her vision becomes blurred, and she feels overwhelmed by a sudden weariness: 'By this stage I can't perform my job properly, and I dare not drive my car.' And so Alison returns to her cigarettes after each attempt to stop. The alternatives as Alison sees them, are, 'Crash my car or get fired from my job.'

Why was giving up for Claudia relatively painless, but insurmountable for Alison? Will your experience be like Claudia's or Alison's? As far as the research goes, the majority of smokers, like Claudia, do find it easy to stop. A minority only experience physical symptoms and substantial difficulty. There is, unfortunately, no way of knowing whether you will be in the majority. And you can't rely on past attempts to gauge how hard it will be. The difficulty you experience depends not only on the body's physical response to cutting off the supply of chemicals in tobacco, but also on your circumstances and frame of mind at the time. In other words, the more stressful your life is, the more aware you will be of being deprived of cigarettes. Alison, for example, sees her 'withdrawal symptoms' as entirely physical in origin. But there are other forces at work. Alison has, for example, noticed that there *is* a time when she can go for longer periods without cigarettes: when she is gardening. Under normal circumstances she smokes a cigarette roughly every half an hour, yet when in the garden she can go without for several hours at a time: 'Gardening is good therapy. It makes me bodily tired, but mentally very much at peace and relaxed,' says Alison. Alison, like most of us, can't afford to spend the whole of her life gardening, and her difficulty in stopping is heightened by the daily stresses of normal working life. It is equally likely, therefore, that if she attempted to stop at a time when she was either away from work, or when pressures on her were minimal, that her 'withdrawal symptoms' could also be minimal.

What is the 'Withdrawal Syndrome'?

The idea of a 'withdrawal syndrome', like the definition of the 'helpless addict', is firmly entrenched in our minds. Yet research shows that **You may not experience a withdrawal syndrome at all**. Although estimates vary, up to half of smokers who stop don't experience withdrawal symptoms.

I think it is more useful to think of the period after stopping in a different way: I would divide the post-smoking phase in two stages of varying length: Stage I is that of the *Reluctant Ex-Smoker*. This is the period immediately after stopping during which you will, not unexpectedly, want or need cigarettes. And the strength of this need will vary from person to person. Stage II is that of the *Nostalgic Ex-Smoker* and follows immediately from Stage I.

Stage I: The Reluctant Ex-Smoker—What to expect

Research shows that ex-smokers experience far fewer disabling symptoms than the spectre of a 'Withdrawal Syndrome' would suggest. Less than 20 per cent experience any restlessness, insomnia or loss of concentration. The most important 'symptom' which emerges from the research is that of *wanting a cigarette*![2]

But this does not mean you should underestimate that need. It can vary from mildly missing cigarettes to a real and urgent craving. The best defence you have against such cravings is to *be prepared for them*. Cravings, as Clara found, for example, come in waves: 'I simply learned to accept that they pass.'

Although it need not necessarily happen, you may experience a series of sensations ranging from the vague and niggling to clearcut physical responses. The commonest feeling, which just over half of ex-smokers experience, is the urge to 'Have something in their mouth,' especially when tense. Second commonest is what researchers describe as 'increased nervousness and irritability' which can mean anything from slight moodiness to frightening mood swings. Abrupt adjustment to life without cigarettes can also make you feel lethargic or shaky and even constipated in the early stages.

How Long Do the Symptoms Last?

The immediate symptoms—if you experience any—usually appear within hours of your last cigarette. They will be most acute during the first 36 hours while your body is still expelling nicotine. Most ex-smokers find that they diminish within a week, though they may recur for a few weeks. If you do find that your mood changes, you will probably feel relatively all right in the mornings, but quite crotchety at night. You can help eliminate nicotine by taking extra vitamin C during this period.

While your body is cleansing itself of the chemicals in tobacco, it is, at the same time, beginning to recover from the damage that smoking may already have done. The repair process starts immediately. But don't expect miracles. If you have abused your lungs and arteries for 10 years or more, it is hardly fair to demand instant recovery. If you already have the early signs of chronic bronchitis—a persistent cough with which you produce a rather unappetising phlegm—don't be surprised if the immediate effect of giving up smoking seems to make you cough more profusely. This is because the phlegm caused by your smoking inevitably gets 'stuck' in your lungs so when you stop smoking, the first step in the recovery process is to cough up that trapped phlegm.

Stage II: The Nostalgic Ex-Smoker

Once over the first few weeks you will reach a new danger period: you are no longer a smoker, but cannot yet regard yourself as safely on the ex-smoker's terrain. You have probably invested a lot of energy and effort into stopping and surviving Stage I. You will—justifiably—feel thoroughly pleased with yourself. In Stage I the novelty and sheer sense of achievement will help cement your resolve to stay off cigarettes. Others will be impressed with your success. Even non-smokers will take notice. But the accolade is short-lived.

As you progress into the world of the ex-smoker your audience—even you—will become less impressed by the impact of your new status. This is the danger period of Stage II, the time during which the rewards of stopping seem dim compared with those of smoking. You are still too close to your old cigarette-smoking status for comfort. And like the ex-alcoholic who gets the bottle of vodka for Christmas, one slip-up and all your effort will be wasted. It is a time when the Group could prove important in helping to revive your flagging determination. Not only will it allow you to voice your doubts, but members will listen avidly to your stories of how you almost succumbed at a party last week, or how you valiantly fought the urge when you had a row with a colleague at work. The group will understand the importance of these continuing victories for you.

118

How Long Does It Take to Become an Ex-Smoker?

Giving up smoking, like any other complex human activity, is a rather enigmatic business. I can't give you a thermometer to gauge your ex-smoker status. But you will know when it has happened. You will stop thinking about cigarettes. You will no longer have to be vigilant over former cigarette cues and temptations. You will no longer even feel smug: just normal. You will become an ex-smoker when cigarettes cease to have any relevance in your life. Researchers themselves do not entirely agree over when to call someone who's given up an ex-smoker. They usually define successful ex-smokers as those who are still off cigarettes a year after they stop. But this is a somewhat arbitrary threshold. The point at which *you* know that *you* will never need another cigarette is entirely individual, and varies enormously. I, for one, knew that after I had weathered the first two months, there was no question of ever going back to cigarettes. In general, about half who stop are likely to return to cigarettes within six months. By nine months, most ex-smokers are 'safe' ex-smokers. But this is not a hard and fast rule—I have known the odd smoker to still feel the need for cigarettes for longer than a year.

Weight Gain—Is It Inevitable?

Contrary to what most smokers think, A GAIN IN WEIGHT IS NOT INEVITABLE on giving up. One third of women, according to the research, do not gain any weight at all. Some actually *lose* weight. But about two-thirds of women who stop smoking do gain a few pounds.[2]

There are several possible factors which can contribute to this. First, and most obvious, food actually tastes better, the ex-smoker's appetite increases, and she eats more. Second, smoking hinders food absorption, and stopping improves it. There is also a possibility that until the ex-smoker adjusts to the improvement, she burns up food less efficiently—which could also contribute to a gain in weight. But by far the most important factor for women is that stopping smoking removes a vital means for both satisfying and controlling hunger (see chapter 5). Which means facing a doubly powerful desire to eat. The woman in this position soon finds herself caught in a vicious circle. Imagine: you stop smoking, and without apparently over-eating, you notice that you have gained a few pounds. This depresses you. You feel out of control, and you eat to console yourself. You gain more weight and begin to feel an increasingly urgent need for cigarettes—which is even more depressing. You then begin to wonder if all the effort was worthwhile . . .

To many women there seem only two ways out of this dilemma: to return to cigarettes, and thus the old mechanism of weight control, or to make a supreme effort to control both your smoking and your eating. Both solutions perpetuate the vicious circle. In the first case, you will be back to square one, only heavier. And in the second, not only will you be diluting the all-important effort of will you need to keep off cigarettes, you will be in the impossible position of curbing two needs which are inextricably bound up with one another.

I could, of course, recommend low calorie diets, or other ways of losing weight, *but I would only be helping you to perpetuate the very pattern you are trying to break*. Instead of automatically struggling with your weight as if it were part of your job description, try, instead, to answer the following questions:

1. How will my life change if I gain a few pounds?
2. Why am I preoccupied with being thin?
3. Whom am I trying to please by striving to stay thin?
4. Is it more important to please others than to restore my health?

I suggest that each member of the group talks about what the consequences of gaining weight will be for her. Will a few pounds *really* make you fat? Will you become a less worthy person? Do you value your body more than anything else about yourself? Do you feel that you have nothing else of value to offer? Your answers will, perhaps, help you to release yourself from a size-10 mental straight jacket.

When Barbara first stopped smoking she couldn't and wouldn't come to terms with gaining weight. Instead, she guarded her despair like a guilty secret. 'I gained half-a-stone in the first month, and another half-a-stone in the next two months. I felt gross and obscene. None of my clothes fitted me. Instead of being pleased with my success in stopping, I became more and more preoccupied with not being able to control my weight. I didn't dare talk to anyone about it—it seemed tantamount to admitting I was a failure. I kept postponing meetings connected with my job because I couldn't face people. I was relieved when my boyfriend and I made love in the dark so that he didn't have to see what I regarded as my mutilated body. I eventually became so depressed that my boyfriend finally forced me to talk about it. Although I don't think he could quite appreciate how I could be obsessed with something so seemingly trivial, he was amazed and hurt that I could think that his feelings for me were as superficial as the fluctuations of a set of bathroom scales. I began to feel increasingly ashamed and appalled that he should have more respect for me than I did for myself. As time went on, I began to feel more confident not only in my ability to stay off cigarettes, which I had, by then, long forgotten—but in *myself as a person*. I eventually stopped trying to starve myself and, after six months, not only was I still off cigarettes, but I was back to my normal weight.'

How They Coped

Although every woman will ultimately find her own way of coping without cigarettes, comparing notes and sharing your experiences with other members of the group will probably help to spur you on as well as giving you a wider range of ideas for how to deal with 'danger spots' if they arise.

Clara

Clara, without being fully aware of it, prepared herself for giving up for nearly a year. First, she switched to a low tar cigarette. She then cut down from 40 to 20 a day. After a while she was almost ready to go the whole way, but she still had to battle with the constant cigarette cues—especially from her heavy-smoking flatmates. She had her last cigarette before she escaped to the country to spend a weekend with some non-smoking relatives. She had almost, but not quite, assured herself that she could succed. For Clara, the final support came from the local group she attended for two months: 'When I arrived at the group meeting I was looking for excuses to start smoking again. But instead I found the confidence I'd needed for so long to actually see it through.'

'I did several things that now seem silly in retrospect, but were desperately important to me then. I made a wall chart, and I charted my progress on six large bits of paper. I covered the walls of my room. My success grew all around me. I used to number each day as I successfully got through it without a cigarette. I remember vividly that the 13th, 14th and 15th days were the hardest. You could tell from the incredibly ornate and tortuous numbering I chalked up on those days. For Clara, Stage I of giving up lasted three weeks. During that time she learned to cope with the waves of cigarette panic that arose with gradually decreasing frequency: 'In those first few weeks I played all sorts of games with myself. I would recoil in mock horror whenever I saw an ashtray in my flat. I would fill it with water and throw it away because I couldn't trust myself yet. The only thing I couldn't stop doing was chewing Fox's Glacier Mints, eating Polos, and chewing gum all day. The only person who was really furious when I stopped smoking was my dentist. And I stayed just about as slim as I was before I stopped.' One of the most difficult things Clara had to face was experiencing the full blast of the volatile feelings she had been able to 'banish' previously with her cigarettes: 'I had to live my life from mood to mood, from moment to moment. Everything seemed to happen in a panic. Once I realised that I could actually work without smoking I knew the panic was over. From then on it became surprisingly easy. It was much easier to *actually* stop than *trying* to stop for years.'

Claudia

Claudia couldn't remember how many failed attempts she had made before she finally succeeded—there were so many. Her doctor's warning that she should stop brought her closer to the final decision, but it was two years before she was finally ready to succeed. Like Clara, Claudia sought the support and encouragement she felt she needed from a local group. After the first meeting she was resolute about stopping—or so she thought. It was, in fact, her last false start. A few hours later that evening she succumbed: 'I was watching this awful play about an alcoholic husband who was beating up his wife. I made myself watch it. I was so desperately trying to keep my mind off cigarettes. It was so horrific, I eventually couldn't bear to watch it without a cigarette. Once I started I couldn't stop: I smoked a storm in bed—which is not unusual for me anyway. I had all those familiar thoughts of being inadequate and useless. Just as I was wallowing in self-pity, I thought to myself: I really will try . . . tomorrow. I put the light out and had another cigarette half an hour later—in sympathy with the seriousness of the decision that faced me in the morning. I then had my very last cigarette and then concealed all the smoking utensils.'

'The next morning I just kept moving, not daring to stop. I

had a few days off work. In the following nights I averaged about an hour's sleep a night. But I was on holiday, and the sleep loss was trivial compared with the immensity of my achievement.'

Claudia's way of dealing with her craving for a cigarette was to immediately fill her mind with something else. She was constantly trying to outwit herself, not letting up for one moment, not running out of alternatives. She developed a set of safe, almost mechanical responses. Take, for example, the day she stopped: 'It was very hot, I was slowly going bananas. It was easy to recognise the signs. I was getting more and more fidgety. I grabbed hold of the carpet sweeper and knocked hell out of the carpet. It made a helluva noise, and it took me hours. The sweat poured off me, but it was terrific. I felt so drained. By the time I'd finished I was too tired to even think about a cigarette.' Claudia rapidly became adept at devising a series of little rituals to foil herself and her cigarette panics: 'Sometimes I'd mechanically go off and make a cup of coffee the moment a cigarette came into my head. I drank so much coffee in those first two weeks I thought I'd explode. It wasn't so much drinking it that was so helpful, but the whole preparation process was somehow reassuring. Getting the milk from the fridge, filling the kettle, spooning out the coffee. Going through those familiar motions soothed me, kept me occupied.'

No sooner out of a crisis, Claudia found herself in another later that day: 'I could feel the agitation welling up again. I had decided to go out that night, because I thought it would do me good, but I wondered how on earth I would deal with it without smoking. I remember getting ready, thinking: How am I going to get through the door, walk to the tube, find my way and cope with all those people. It was a social evening and I didn't have a cigarette I could hide behind . . . I decided not to say a word [about stopping] to anybody. I kept saying yes to more coffee, wondering how I didn't spill the cup each time, because my hands were all over the place. But it worked: not only did I survive, nobody seemed to notice my difficulty.'

After the first 36 hours Claudia became good at dealing with her new status. She realised that it wasn't so bad after all. Having very rapidly overcome what she saw as the physical part of her smoking, she then had to come more slowly to terms with the emotional part: 'I know that I am a very needful person. The emotional need for cigarettes was far greater for me than any physical need. While I knew that cigarettes were always a response to intense feelings, I tried to keep everything at low key. I couldn't allow myself to get angry or upset because I knew I would immediately say: Sod it, I'm going to have a cigarette. So I tried to avoid conflict in the early days, keeping as placid and calm as possible.'

As the weeks went by, and Claudia's confidence grew, she became less afraid to express herself more freely. She felt she had finally reached a point 'when it was no longer necessary to deal with my problems either by smoking or other chemical aids. . .I'm almost surprised now when people ask me how the smoking is going. I feel like saying: but I'm a non-smoker *now*.'

Useful Organisations

ASH National Office
27–35 Mortimer Street
London W1N 7RJ

Tel: 01-637 9843

Health Education Council
78 New Oxford Street
London WC1A 1AH

Tel: 01-637 1881

Scottish Health Education Group
Health Education Centre
Woodburn House
Canaan Lane
Edinburgh EH10 4SG

Tel: 031-447 8044

ASH in Northern Ireland
Ulster Cancer Foundation
40 Eglantine Avenue
Belfast BT9 6DX

Tel: 0232-663281

Scottish Committee ASH
at Royal College of Physicians
9 Queen Street
Edinburgh EH12 1JQ

Tel: 031-225 4725

ASH in Wales
c/o Naomi King
92 Cathedral Road
Cardiff
Wales

North West ASH
c/o Dr Satinder Lal
Bury General Hospital
Walmersley Road
Bury BL9 6PG

Northern ASH
c/o Mrs Moses
Newcastle-upon-Tyne Polytechnic
Coach Lane Campus
Newcastle-upon-Tyne
NE7 7XA

West Midlands ASH
c/o Dr John Roberts
West Midlands RHA
Arthur Thompson House
146/150 Hagley Road
Birmingham B16 9PA

East Anglia ASH
c/o Dr Noel Olsen
District Community Physician
Addenbrooke's Hospital
Cambridge CB2 2QQ

Suffolk ASH
c/o R. W. Rossington
Area Health Education Officer
Suffolk AHA
P.O. Box 55
Ipswich IP3 8NN

Solent ASH
c/o Dr Denis Hilton
Dept of Community Medicine
Lombard Street
Portsmouth PO1 2JQ

References

The place of publication is London, unless otherwise stated.

2. Today's Epidemic pages 11–17

1. M. J. Wilson, *Statistics of Smoking in the United Kingdom*, Research Paper I, 7th ed. Tobacco Research Council, 1976, pp.40–41.
2. *National Opinion Poll Survey*, May/June 1980, Department of Health and Social Security, unpublished.
3. 'Cigarette smoking: an extract from the *General Household Survey* (1978)', *OPCS Monitor*, 7 August 1979.
4. G. F. Todd, 'Cigarette consumption per adult of each sex in various countries', *Journal of Epidemiology and Community Health*, vol.32, 1978, pp.289–93.
5. *Cigarette Smoking Among Teenagers and Young Women*, Washington D.C.: National Cancer Institute in cooperation with the American Cancer Society, 1977, pp.5–6.
6. M. J. Wilson, *op.cit.* pp.52–55.
7. B. Benjamin, *Tobacco Smoking in the World*, Geneva: World Health Organisation, Document CVD/S/EC/78.23, 1978, p.15.
8. N. J. Gray and D. J. Hill, 'Patterns of tobacco smoking in Australia', *Medical Journal of Australia*, vol.2, 3 September 1977, pp.327–28.
9. *Smoking Habits of Canadians 1975*, Canada: Department of National Health and Welfare, Technical Report Series No. 7, December 1977.
10. M. Rimpela, *Changes in Viewpoints Concerning the Hazards of Smoking and Smoking Habits in Connection with the Implementation of the Tobacco Act in Finland*, Helsinki: National Health Board of Finland, 1978.
11. F. Buhl, *Quelles sont les difficultés recontrées dans l'application de la réglementation relative a la lutte contre le tabagisme en France?*, paper given at the Fourth World Conference on Smoking and Health, 1979.
12. D. R. Hay, 'Cigarette smoking in New Zealand: results from the 1976 Population Census', *New Zealand Medical Journal*, vol.88 no.618, 23 August 1978.
13. *ASH Bulletin*, no.15, 9 November 1978, p.4.
14. L. Ramstrom and A. Barroll, personal communication from *NTS Investigation of Smoking Habits in Sweden in 1976 and 1977*.
15. M. J. Wilson, *op.cit.* pp.40–41.
16. *The Health Consequences of Smoking for Women: A Report of the Surgeon General*, Washington D.C.: US Department of Health, Education and Welfare, 1980, p.23.

17. K. Bjartreit, 'Scandinavian Strategies', from a paper given at ASH 10th Anniversary Conference, 1981, unpublished.

18. *The Health Consequences of Smoking for Women, op.cit.*

19. N. C. Delarue, 'A study in smoking withdrawal', *Canadian Journal of Public Health,* vol.64, March/April 1973, pp.S5–S19

20. R. A. Eisinger, 'Psychosocial predictors of smoking recidivism', *Journal of Health and Social Behaviour,* vol.12, December 1971, pp.355–62.

21. M. E. Thompson, *Statistics of Smoking in Canada,* unpublished, pp.88–109.

22. *ibid.* pp.90–93.

23. J. L. Schwarz and M. Dubitsky, 'Changes in anxiety, mood and self-esteem resulting from an attempt to stop smoking', *American Journal of Psychiatry,* vol.124, 11 May 1968, pp.138–42.

24. M. Dubitsky and J. L. Schwarz, 'Ego resiliency, ego control and smoking cessation', *Journal of Psychology,* vol.70, 1968, pp.27–33.

25. M. E. Thompson, *op.cit.* pp.88–93.

26. J. S. Guilford, 'Group versus individual treatment initiative in the cessation of smoking', *Journal of Applied Psychology,* vol.56 no.2, 1972, pp.162–67.

27. M. E. Thompson, *op.cit.* pp.23–88.

28. *Smoking and Health: A Report of the Surgeon General,* Washington D.C.: US Department of Health, Education and Welfare, 1979, pp.A16–A17.

29. *Smoking Or Health: A Report of the Royal College of Physicians,* Pitman Medical, 1977, pp.16–20.

30. E. Wynder, 'Epidemiology of smoking habits and prospects for reduction in risk for sub-populations of smokers', awaiting publication.

31. *The Health Consequences of Smoking for Women, op.cit.* pp.296–97.

32. Wynder, *op.cit.*

33. *Smoking and Health, op.cit.* p.A16.

34. M. E. Thompson, *op.cit.* pp.88–109.

35. D. Horn, *Adult Use of Tobacco,* Washington D.C.: US Department of Health, Education and Welfare, June 1976, pp.IV-2 to IV-4.

36. *National Opinion Poll Survey,* Department of Health and Social Security, November/December 1978, unpublished.

37. 'Cigarette smoking: an extract from the *General Household Survey* (1978)', *op.cit.*

38. H. Cuckle, personal communication from preliminary findings of the *Reports Action* study.

39. *The Health Consequences of Smoking for Women, op.cit.* pp.306–17.

40. N. C. Delarue, *op.cit.* pp.S16–S17.

41. *Mortality Statistics,* Office of Population Censuses and Surveys, 1977.

42. 'Mortality statistics', *The Registrar General (Scotland) Annual Report,* 1977, Part I.

43. *Annual Report of the Registrar General (Northern Ireland),* 1977.

44. *The Health Consequences of Smoking for Women, op.cit.* p.112.

45. B. Benjamin, 'Trends and differentials in lung cancer mortality', *World Health Statistics Report,* vol.30 no.2, 1977, pp.118–45.

46. W. C. Chan *et al,* 'Bronchial carcinoma in Hong Kong 1976–77', *British Journal of Cancer,* vol.39, 1979, pp. 182–92.

47. T. Hirayama, 'Non-Smoking Wives of Heavy Smoking Husbands have a

127

higher Risk of Lung-Cancer: a Study from Japan', *British Medical Journal*, vol.282, 17 January 1981, pp. 183–5.

48. 'Deaths by cause', *OPCS Monitor*, DH2 80/3, 2 September 1980.

49. *The Health Consequences of Smoking for Women*, *op.cit.* p.88.

50. V. Beral and C. R. Kay, 'Royal College of General Practitioners' oral contraception study', *Lancet*, vol.2 no.8041, 1977, pp.727–31.

51. S. Shapiro *et al*, 'Oral contraceptive use in relation to myocardial infarction', *Lancet*, vol.1 no.8119, April 1979, pp.743–77.

52. D. B. Pettiti and J. Wingerd, 'Use of oral contraceptives, cigarette smoking and risk of subarachnoid haemorrhage', *Lancet*, vol.2 no.8083, 29 July 1978, pp.234–35.

53. 'Deaths by cause', *op.cit.*

3. Tomorrow's Casualties pages 18–22

1. I. Waldron, 'Why do women live longer than men?', *Social Science and Medicine*, vol.10, 1976, pp.352–62.

2. *Smoking and Health: A Report of the Surgeon General*, Washington D.C.: US Department of Health, Education and Welfare, 1979, pp.5-16 & 5-17.

3. *The Health Consequences of Smoking for Women: A Report of the Surgeon General*, Washington D.C.: US Department of Health, Education and Welfare, 1980, p.110.

4. 'Lung cancer: female fatalities increase', *Cancer Topics*, vol.2 no.9, Nov/Dec 1979, p.1.

5. J. Peto, *The health effects of smoking in women*, paper given at the Fourth World Conference on Smoking and Health: Stockholm, unpublished.

6. N. Rawson, personal communication of linear regression analysis from mortality data for breast cancer and lung cancer compiled by the Office of Population Censuses and Surveys, unpublished.

7. S. G. Haynes *et al*, 'The relationship of psychosocial factors to coronary heart disease in the Framingham study', *American Journal of Epidemiology*, vol.3 no.1, 1980, pp.37–38.

8. *ibid.*

9. 'OCs: update on usage, safety and side effects', *Population Report*, series A no.5, January 1979.

10. *The Health Consequences of Smoking for Women*, *op.cit.* p.296.

11. *ASH Bulletin*, no.11, 13 September 1978, p.5.

12. B. Benjamin, *Tobacco Smoking in the World*, Geneva: World Health Organisation, document CVD/S/EC78.23.

13. *Cancer Incidence and Mortality in the United States, 1973–76*, S.E.E.R. Programme, Washington D.C.: US Department of Health, Education and Welfare, 1978.

14. 'International news', *Tobacco Reporter*, vol.105 no.3, pp.13–14.

15. *ibid.* p.13.

16. M. Muller, *Tobacco and the Third World: Tomorrow's Epidemic?*, War on Want, 1978.

17. *Financial Times*, 19 July 1980.

18. P. C. Gupta and F. S. Melita, 'The dynamics of tobacco habits in the rural Indian population', paper given at the 17th Asian Cancer Conference, December 1979, unpublished.

19. B. Benjamin, *op.cit.* p.20.

20. *Tobacco Reporter, op.cit.* p.13.

21. B. Wickstrom, *Cigarette Marketing in the Third World: A Study of Four Centres*, University of Gothenburg, 1979.

22. D. J. Joly, 'Cigarette smoking in Latin America: a study of eight countries', *Pan American Health Organisation Bulletin*, vol.9 no.4, 1975, pp.329–44.

23. B. Benjamin, 'Trends and differentials in lung cancer mortality', *World Health Statistics Report*, vol.30 no.2, 1977, pp.118–45.

4. Why Women Smoke—The Experts' View pages 23–29

1. B. R. Bewley, *A prevalance study in final year primary school children (10–11 years) and some factors associated with smoking at this age*, M.Sc. thesis: University of London, 1971.

2. B. R. Bewley and J. M. Bland, 'Academic performance and social factors related to cigarette smoking by school children', *British Journal of Social and Preventive Medicine*, vol.31, 1977, pp.18–24.

3. *ibid.*

4. J. M. Bynner, *The Young Smoker*, government social survey, HMSO, 1969.

5. B. R. Bewley *et al*, 'Teachers' smoking', *Journal of Epidemiology and Community Health*, vol.33, 1979, pp.219–22.

6. F. E. Wright, *Report of the survey evaluation of the 1979 national education week on smoking of the Canadian Council on Smoking and Health*, unpublished.

7. *Smoking Or Health: A Report of the Royal College of Physicians*, Pitman Medical, 1977.

8. *ibid.* p.45.

9. *ibid.* p.45.

10. D. G. Williams, 'Effects of cigarette smoking on immediate memory and performance in different kinds of smoker', *British Journal of Psychology*, vol.71, 1980, pp.83–90.

11. M. A. H. Russell *et al*, 'Effects of nicotine chewing gum on smoking behaviour as an aid to cigarette withdrawal', *British Medical Journal*, vol.2, 1976, pp.391–93.

12. H. Ashton *et al*, 'Self-titration by cigarette smokers', *British Medical Journal*, vol.2, 1979, 357–60.

13. R. G. Rawbone, 'Self-titration by cigarette smokers', *British Medical Journal*, 22 September 1979, pp.731–32.

14. R. Kumar *et al*, 'Is nicotine important in tobacco smoking?', *Clinical Pharmacology and Therapeutics*, vol.21 no.5, 1976, pp.520–29.

15. *Smoking and Health: A Report of the Surgeon General*, Washington D.C.: US Department of Health, Education and Welfare, 1979, pp.15-13 to 15-18.

16. *ibid.* pp.16-14 to 16-18.

17. *Smoking Or Health, op.cit.* pp.105–7.

18. A. Burt *et al*, 'Smoking after myocardial infarction', *Lancet*, 23 February 1974, vol.1 no.7852, pp.304–6.

19. *Smoking and Health, op.cit.* pp.18-5 to 18-9.

20. *ibid.* pp.18-5 to 18-9.

21. *ibid.* pp.18-5 to 18-8.

22. S. Tomkins, 'Theoretical implications and guidelines to future research on smoking', in B. Mausner and E. Platt (eds.), *Behavioural Aspects of Smoking: A Conference Report*, Health Education Monographs, supplement no.2, 1966.

23. F. F. Ikard *et al*, 'A scale to differentiate between types of smoking as related to the management of affect', *International Journal of the Addictions*, vol.4 no.4, December 1969, pp.649–59.

24. F. F. Ikard and S. Tomkins, 'The experience of affect as a determinant of smoking behaviour', *Journal of Abnormal Psychology*, vol.81, no.2, 1973, pp.172–81.

25. M. A. H. Russell and J. Peto, 'The classification of smoking by factorial structure of motives', *The Journal of the Royal Statistics Society*, series A (general), vol.137, part 3, 1974, p.313–46.

26. W. Fee, 'Searching for the simple answer to cure the smoking habit', *Health and Social Service Journal*, 18 February 1977, pp.292–93.

5. Why Do Women Smoke? pages 29–39

1. J. S. Tamerin, 'The psychodynamics of quitting smoking in a group', *American Journal of Psychiatry*, vol.129 no.5, November 1972, pp.589–95.

2. C. Bailey, 'Smoking', *Ms London*, 21 July 1975.

3. E. Wynder, P. L. Kaufman and R. L. Lesser, 'A short-term follow-up on ex-cigarette-smokers', *American Review of Respiratory Diseases*, vol.96, 1967, pp.645–55.

4. P. H. Blitzer, A. A. Rimm and E. E. Giefer, 'The effect of cessation of smoking on body weight in 57,032 women: cross-sectional and longitudinal analyses', *Journal of Chronic Diseases*, vol. 30, 1977, pp.415–29.

5. J. L. Schwarz and M. Dubitsky, *Requisites for success in smoking withdrawal. Current Research*, 1968, pp.231–47. (The basic methodology used in this research is given in 'The smoking control research project: purpose, design and initial results', *Psychological Reports*, vol.20, 1967, pp.367–76.)

6. *National Opinion Poll Survey*, Department of Health and Social Security, Nov/Dec 1978, unpublished.

6. A Society that Keeps Women Smoking pages 40–45

1. S. V. Zagona and L. A. Zurcher, 'An analysis of some psychosocial variables associated with cigarette smoking in a college sample', *Psychological Reports*, vol.17, 1965, pp.967–78.

2. L. P. Bozzetti, 'Group psychotherapy with addicted smokers', *Psychotherapy and Psychosomatics*, vol.20, 1972, pp.172–75.

3. L. G. Reeder, 'Socio-cultural factors in the etiology of smoking behaviour: an assessment', *National Institute of Drug Abuse Research Monograph Series No.17*, Washington D.C.: US Department of Health, Education and Welfare, 1977, pp.186–200.

4. J. R. Fisher, 'Sex differences in smoking dynamics', *Journal of Health and Social Behaviour*, vol.17, June 1976, pp.155–62.

5. *Cigarette Smoking Among Teenagers and Young Women*, Washington D.C.: US Department of Health, Education and Welfare, 1977.

6. P. P. Aitken, *Ten to Fourteen Year Olds and Alcohol: A Development Study in the Central Region of Scotland*, Edinburgh: Scottish Home and Health Department Health Education Unit, HMSO vol.III, 1978.

7. B. R. Bewley and J. M. Bland, 'The child's image of a young smoker', *Health Education Journal*, vol.37 no.4, pp.236–41.

8. *Taskforce on Tobacco and Cancer*, New York: American Cancer Society, 1977, pp.30–43.

9. B. R. Bewley and J. M. Bland, 'Academic performance and social factors related to cigarette smoking by school children', *British Journal of Social and Preventive Medicine*, vol.31, 1977, pp.18–24.

10. Personal communication from MIND, National Association for Mental Health, UK.

11. *The Health Consequences of Smoking for Women: A Report of the Surgeon General*, Washington D.C.: US Department of Health, Education and Welfare, 1980, pp.259–61.

12. *ibid.*

13. *Taskforce on Tobacco and Cancer, op.cit.* pp.30–43.

14. C. E. Lewis and M. A. Lewis, 'The potential impact of sexual equality on health', *New England Journal of Medicine*, vol.297 no.16, 20 October 1977, pp.863–69.

15. L. W. Hoffman, 'Early childhood experiences and women's achievement motives', *Journal of Social Issues*, vol.28 no.2, 1972, pp.129–155.

16. D. Weatherley, 'Some personality correlates of the ability to stop smoking cigarettes', *Journal of Consulting Psychology*, vol.29 no.5, 1965, pp.483–85.

17. E. Lenney, 'Women's self-confidence in achievement settings', *Psychological Bulletin*, vol.84 no.1, January 1977, pp.1–13.

18. I. H. Frieze *et al*, *Women and Sex Roles: A Social Psychological Perspective*, New York: W. W. Norton, 1978.

19. S. Orbach, *Fat Is a Feminist Issue*, Paddington Press, 1977.

7. A Question of Conflict pages 46–50

1. *The Health Consequences of Smoking for Women: A Report of the Surgeon General*, Washington D.C.: US Department of Health, Education and Welfare, 1980, p.305.

8. Hospitals—A Microcosm of Male Dominance
pages 50–56

1. *Smoking and Professional People*, Department of Health and Social Security, 1977.

2. *ibid.*

3. *Smoking and Nurses: Proceedings of a One-Day Symposium*, Scotland: Action on Smoking and Health, 1979.

4. *The Health Consequences of Smoking for Women: A Report of the Surgeon General*, Washington D.C.: US Department of Health, Education and Welfare, 1980, pp. 329–32.

5. R. J. Kirby *et al*, 'Smoking in nurses', *Medical Journal of Australia*, vol.2 no.23, 1976, p.864.

6. *The Health Consequences of Smoking for Women, op.cit.* pp.329–32.

7. W. P. Small and L. Tucker, 'Smoking habits of hospital nurses', *Nursing Times*, November 1978, p.1878.

8. W. G. Adams, 'Survey of tobacco and alcohol use among undergraduates', *Medical Journal of Australia*, vol.2 no.3, 11 August 1979, p.160.

9. I. C. McManus *et al*, 'Smoking behaviour in medical students', *British Medical Journal*, vol.1 no.6106, 1978, p.175.
10. *Smoking and Professional People, op.cit.*
11. *Smoking and Health: A Report of the Surgeon General*, Washington D.C.: US Department of Health, Education and Welfare, 1979, pp.22-5 to 22-11.
12. *The Health Consequences of Smoking for Women, op.cit.*
13. P. W. Wilkinson and L. Tylden-Pattenson, '*Smoking habits of nurses within the Leeds Area Health Authority (teaching)*', awaiting publication.
14. B. Ehrenreich, 'Is success dangerous to your health?', *Ms*, May 1979.
15. *Smoking and Professional People, op.cit.*
16. *The Health Consequences of Smoking for Women, op.cit.* p.330.
17. D. R. Hay, 'Cigarette smoking by New Zealand doctors: results from the 1976 census', *New Zealand Medical Journal*, vol.91 no.658, 23 April 1980, pp.285–89.
18. A. Knopf Elkind, 'Nurses, smoking and cancer prevention', *International Journal of Health Education*, vol.22 no.2, 1979, pp.92–101.
19. H. Westling-Wikstrand *et al*, 'Some characteristics related to the career status of women physicians', *Johns Hopkins Medical Journal*, vol.127 no.5, November 1970, pp.213–86.
20. *ibid*.

9. The Ladykillers—US Style pages 56–62

1. *Federal Trade Commission: Report to Congress*, 1978.
2. *Advertising Age*, 7 May 1979.
3. *Federal Trade Commission, op.cit.*
4. R. Scott, *The Female Consumer*, Associated Business Programmes, 1976, pp.171–72.
5. *Federal Trade Commission, op.cit.*
6. *Tobacco Reporter*, December 1977.
7. *Advertising and Women*, National Advertising Review Board, March 1975.
8. 'Why Philip Morris Thrives', *Business Week*, 27 January 1973, pp.48–54.
9. *Advertising Age*, 23 August 1976.
10. *Advertising Age*, 11 December 1979.
11. *Advertising Age*, 23 August 1976.
12. *ibid*.

10. British Cunning pages 63–69

1. M. Dean, 'Blowing away smoke screens', *The Guardian*, 4 January 1980.
2. *Smoking and Health Now: A Report of the Royal College of Physicians*, Pitman Medical, 1971.
3. *Smoking Or Health: A Report of the Royal College of Physicians*, Pitman Medical, 1977.
4. *The British Code of Advertising Practice*, Advertising Standards Authority, Appendix M, August 1975.
5. *The British Code of Advertising Practice*, Advertising Standards Authority, Appendix M, 1977.
6. *National Opinion Poll Survey*, Department of Health and Social Security, May 1978, unpublished.
7. *Ms London*, 6 December 1976.
8. R. Moyle, parliamentary question, *Hansard*, 13 December 1976.

9. *The British Code of Advertising Practice*, 1977, *op.cit.*
10. *Tobacco International*, 22 December 1978.
11. R. Scott, *The Female Consumer*, Associated Business Programmes, 1976, p.155.
12. *Retail Business*, vol.147, May 1970, p.3.
13. *Tobacco*, December 1978.
14. *ibid.*
15. *Tobacco International*, *op.cit.*
16. R. Scott, *op.cit.* pp.73–75.
17. A. B. Atkinson and J. L. Skegg, 'Anti-smoking publicity and the demand for tobacco in the UK', *Manchester School*, vol.41, 1973, pp.265–82.
18. *Smoking and Health Now*, *op.cit.*

11. The Health Educators pages 69–74

1. Editorial, 'Cigarette smoking and spontaneous abortion', *British Medical Journal*, vol.1 no.6108, 4 February 1978, pp.259–60.
2. Editorial, 'ASH', *Journal of the Royal College of General Practitioners*, vol.21, 1971, pp.185–86.
3. N. Hodgkinson, 'Twenty ways to help your husband avoid a heart attack', *Daily Mail*, 21 March 1979.
4. J. Stephenson, 'Girls can stop the smokers', *Daily Mail*, 14 September 1972.
5. *Women Are Kicking the Cigarette Habit*, leaflet, New York: American Lung Association, 1978.
6. A. Yarrow, *So Now You Know About Smoking*, a *Family Doctor* booklet, the British Medical Association.
7. 'Smoked out girls?', *Daily Express*, 3 December 1975.
8. *Smoking in Pregnancy*, Scottish Health Education Unit, proposals for publicity programme, unpublished.
9. Personal communication from the Health Education Council.
10. Communications Research Limited, '*The 1974 anti-smoking campaign in pregnancy: a study of the pregnant nude*', unpublished.
11. D. H. Taylor and M. Robinson, '*Smoking in pregnancy, an intervention study*', commissioned by the Health Education Council, unpublished.
12. Communications Research Limited, '*A qualitative study on attitudes towards a campaign approach*', unpublished.
13. Communications Research Limited, '*Anti-smoking in Pregnancy: a study of four campaign approaches*', unpublished.
14. 'Tobacco—hazards to health and human reproduction', *Population Reports*, series L, no.1, March 1979, pp.L16–17.
15. *The Health Consequences of Smoking for Women: A Report of the Surgeon General*, Washington D.C.: US Department of Health, Education and Welfare, 1980, pp.211–14.
16. *ibid*, pp.117–19.
17. 'Tobacco—hazards to health and human reproduction', *op.cit.* p.L17.
18. *Target Five—The First Two Years*, New York: American Cancer Society, 1980.

12. The Political Activists pages 74–80

1. *World Conference on Smoking and Health*, New York: National Interagency Council on Smoking and Health, 1967.

2. M. Daube, '*Summing up of the Fourth World Conference on Smoking and Health*', unpublished.

3. C. M. Fletcher and D. Horn, *Smoking and Health*, reproduced from the 23rd World Health Assembly proceedings by the Department of Health and Social Security, Scottish Home and Health Department, Welsh Office, 1971.

4. *Smoking and its Effects on Health*, Geneva: WHO Technical Report, series no.568, 1975.

5. *Smoking and Health: Report of the Advisory Committee to the Surgeon General of the Public Health Service*, Washington D.C.: US Department of Health, Education and Welfare, 1964.

6. *The Health Consequences of Smoking*, Washington D.C.: US Department of Health, Education and Welfare, 1973, pp.99–125.

7. *Smoking and Health: A Report of the Surgeon General*, Washington D.C.: US Department of Health, Education and Welfare, 1979.

8. *Fact or Fancy?*, Washington D.C.: The Tobacco Institute, 1978.

9. J. A. Califano, Jr., address to the youth conference of the National Interagency Council on Smoking and Health, April 1979.

10. *ibid*.

11. *Smoking and Health: A Report of the Royal College of Physicians*, Pitman Medical, 1962.

12. *Smoking Or Health: A Report of the Royal College of Physicians*, Pitman Medical, 1977.

13. *ibid*.

14. Sir George Young, answer to parliamentary question, *Hansard*, 3 April 1980, cols.378–80.

15. *First Report from the Expenditure Committee, Session 1976–77, Preventive Medicine*, vol.I, HMSO, 1977, paragraphs 143–61.

16. Lord Leatherdale, *Hansard*, vol.405, 14 February 1980, cols.316–20.

17. A. Phillips and J. Rakusen (eds.), *Our Bodies Ourselves*, Harmondsworth: Penguin, 1979.

18. E.C. Smeal, testimony before the Sub-Committee on Health and Scientific Research of the Committee on Labor and Human Resources in the United States Senate, Washington D.C., August 1979.

19. S. Berlin, '*Smoking and the women's movement*', unpublished paper given at workshop on smoking and health, sponsored by the Canadian Council on Smoking and Health, the Ontario Interagency Council on Smoking and Health and the Department of National Health and Welfare, Canada, 1977.

14. Why Should I Stop? pages 84–93

If you want to read in more depth about the effects of smoking on health, the following references give comprehensive information about the risks discussed in chapters 1 and 2.

1. *The Health Consequences of Smoking for Women: A Report of the Surgeon General*, Washington D.C.: US Department of Health, Education and Welfare, 1980.

2. *Smoking Or Health: A Report of the Royal College of Physicians*, Pitman Medical, 1977.

3. *Smoking and Health: A Report of the Surgeon General*, Washington D.C.: US Department of Health, Education and Welfare, 1979.

4. R. Peto, 'Possible ways of explaining to ordinary people the quantitative dangers of smoking', *Health Education Journal*, vol.39 no.2, 1980, pp.45–46.
5. 'Tobacco—hazards to health and human reproduction', *Population Reports*, series L no.1, March 1979.
6. 'Oral contraceptives: update on usage, safety and side effects', *Population Reports*, series A no.5, January 1979.
7. V. Beral, 'Reproductive mortality', *British Medical Journal*, vol.2, 1979, pp.632–34.
8. K. Fogelman, 'Smoking in pregnancy and subsequent development of the child', *Child Care, Health and Development*, vol.6, 1980, pp.233–49.

15. Will I Get More out of Stopping than Going on Smoking? pages 93–99

1. E. Wynder *et al*, 'A short-term follow-up study on ex-cigarette smokers', *American Review of Respiratory Diseases*, vol.96, 1967, pp.645–55.

16. Have I the Confidence to Stop? pages 100–102

1. The basis for the self-confidence questionnaire was provided by the following two sources: the *Rosenberg Self-Esteem Scale*; and the *Smokers' Self-Testing Kit*, Scotland: Scottish Health Education Unit, 1976.

17. How Do I Stop? pages 103–111

1. E. Gritz, 'Women and smoking: a realistic appraisal', in *Progress in Smoking Cessation: Proceedings of the International Conference on Smoking Cessation*, New York: American Cancer Society, 1977.
2. N. C. Delarue, 'A study in smoking withdrawal', *Canadian Journal of Public Health*, vol.64, 1973, pp.S5–S19.

18. Coping pages 114–124

1. M. Raw *et al*, 'Comparison of nicotine chewing gum and psychological treatments for dependent smokers', *British Medical Journal*, vol.281 no.6238, pp.481–82.
2. E. Wynder *et al, op.cit.*